D1118167

Breaking
the
Prayer
Barrier

Getting Through to God

Michael Baughen

Harold Shaw Publishers
Wheaton, Illinois

This Book
presented to the

CHURCH
LIBRARY

by

Sharon Bradley

Code 4386-21, No. 1, Broadman Supplies, Nashville, Tenn. Printed in USA

Printed in the United States of America

Library of Congress Cataloging in Publication Data

Baughen, Michael A.
    Breaking the prayer barrier.

    1. Prayer. I. Title.
BV215.B38   248.3'2   81-5342
ISBN 0-87788-688-1 (pbk.)   AACR2

90   89   88   87   86   85   84   83   82   81
10   9   8   7   6   5   4   3   2   1

Contents

FOREWORD

Prayer is the measure of the man, spiritually. "What a man is alone on his knees before God," said Murray McCheyne, "that he is, and no more." That cuts most of us down to size! Our era is peopled by lively dwarf Christians with cheerful small souls. The liveliness and cheerfulness are admirable, but our stunted stature is not. Too many of us are cases of arrested spiritual development. Our "superspiritual" naivete and childishness makes us brittle under pressure, unstable when allured and downright unintelligent when facing problems. We are half-baked. What is our trouble? Basically, our problem is the way we haven't prayed.

Every Christian's prayer life, like every good marriage, has in it common factors about which we can generalize, and unique elements which no other Christian's prayer life quite matches. You are you, and I am I, and since we each must find our own way with God, no book on prayer can work for us like a do-it-yourself manual or cookbook, whose publishers tell us that if we follow the instructions exactly we can't go wrong. In relationships—and prayer is a relationship—it is never like that. Books on prayer, like marriage manuals and guides to parenting, are meant rather to strike sparks off our imaginations (by which I mean the creative as distinct from analytical aspect of our minds) about things we can try which we never before thought of trying. But how you go at them will be up to you, and however often you read the book you still will only learn by doing. In prayer, for instance, as in other close relationships, some folk talk more, some less; some are constantly vocal, which is right for them, while for others being still and contemplating God and his works (as one contemplates scenery) is central. Within the biblical guidelines each of us has to find out by experiment how he or she should pray. We only learn to pray by praying.

Prayer has to be a dogged discipline or it would always get crowded out (Satan would see to that); but true prayer is not a dull routine. A Christian's prayer life grows out of a special sort of love affair with the Father and the Son through the Spirit, with child-parent and wife-husband relationships in this world as models, and the essence of such relationships is spontaneity within the proper guidelines. We say and do what expresses our appreciation of the other party and our gratitude for love given, and go on from there with nothing that is merely mechanical entering in at any stage, even if the things we say (in this case, prayers) are things we have often said before. If there is love in our hearts, the meaning will be fresh every time. Such is prayer. It is the fellowship of heaven starting now. We Christians are like lovers whose beloved (Christ) is away but communicates with us by letter (the Bible), while we can converse with him on the phone (prayer). One day we shall see him and communicate face to face, but for the present this is how our relationship with him must proceed.

The ministry of the indwelling Holy Spirit in our prayer life is a constant divine mystery. Paul tells us that the Spirit prompts us to call the Creator Father, and that when we do not know how to pray for ourselves the Spirit prays for us, within us, with unutterable groaning. Also it is the Spirit who in our own petitions and intercessions crystallizes our sense of what specifically to ask for as we spread situations of need before God and seek to view them in his presence in the light of Holy Scripture. Getting our petitions from God in this way, so that we can then present them to him in the confidence that it is his will, not ours, is a major part of the life of prayer. Then the Spirit will keep alive in our hearts the confidence that this or that petition is one which God himself has moved us to make, and that confidence will sustain us when it is our part to pray and not faint over long periods while seemingly nothing happens, or the situation of need gets worse rather than better.

This wise, warm-hearted, down-to-earth book which my friend Michael Baughen has written could greatly enrich our praying and thereby get us growing again. I hope it will. It did me good to read it; I hope it will do good to many more.

James I. Packer

PREFACE

In the first four months of 1978 at All Souls, Langham Place, a series of sermons was preached, entitled "Business with God in Prayer." It had a considerable effect on both the preachers and the hearers. Because the church has a Team Ministry, the series was shared with me by Graham Claydon and Andrew Cornes, with one sermon by John Stott. We all learned from one another and I readily acknowledge the benefit I received from my colleagues' ministry, which is bound to be reflected in the contents of this book. After the series I "went back to square one" and thought through the whole subject again, at some length, in preparation for conference ministry. The conference addresses that resulted have led to this book. I am grateful to all who have helped me through the years, not least in the matter of prayer for me and my work. I am grateful to my present colleagues at All Souls—John Stott, Graham Claydon, Andrew Cornes, Richard Inwood and Roger Simpson—and for all they teach me in the work of the ministry. I am grateful too for the stimulus, vitality, support, and fellowship of the members of the church family at All Souls, a church family that has prayer as the central hub of its life, and I thank them for all they have taught and are still teaching me about prayer.

My warm thanks also to David Winter for his editorial encouragement, to Pippa Dobson, Susan Rybarchyk and Vivienne Curry for typing the manuscript, to Harold Shaw Publishers for publishing it and especially to my wife, Myrtle, for all her help and encouragement.

Michael Baughen

1
BREAKING THE PRAYER BARRIER

CHAPTER 1

GO
BACK
TO *START*

"LET'S START AT THE VERY BEGINNING—it's a very good place to start!" That wise advice for learning the sound of music also holds true for learning how to pray.

You know how it is when you come into the family room: your family is engrossed in a television drama, but you have come in half way through. "Who's that?" you ask; "Why is he running? What is the girl doing with the tape-recorder?" The rest of the family shuts you up. They *know* what's going on and they don't want to miss anything by stopping to explain the story to you. Their understanding stems from the fact that they were in on the plot from the beginning. Your confusion stems from coming in half way through.

We will only understand prayer if we start at the beginning—and that means starting with God. Most of us start too far along the line, in the middle of "the action"—with ourselves. A child does that. The world revolves around him. If he does not get what he wants, he yells or sulks. People are there to serve him, feed him, give him money to spend, love and help him. He is the center of the world.

Where is the center?
I had not realized how we all think like this, even nationally, until I traveled and saw published maps of the world, in the United States with the Americas depicted in the center, in Australia with Australia central, and in Britain with Britain central. We all look out on the world from our own center.

In adult life we are still children in many ways, even though we may be more sophisticated and subtle about it! We are standing in line waiting for a bus. There are fifteen people in the line, we are ninth, and the bus is almost full. How many are we concerned should get on the bus—15 or 9?

It is this attitude that is often reflected in our prayer. In one sense, it is perfectly natural that we should share our needs with our God. After all, we *are* his children by faith in Christ. So isn't it good that Jerry should pray about his new job; that Jackie should pray about the exams she is facing; that Jonathan should pray about his deep longing to be married; that Jill should pray for snow for her ski vacation; that Jean should pray for the success of her gall bladder operation; that Jim should pray for protection as he sets out on a long and dangerous journey; that Joanie should pray for success as she looks for a new car? Yes, it *is* natural for us to pray about such things—as children sharing our needs with our Father.

But it is not stage one. If we start there we get ourselves into all sorts of problems, which can result in loss of faith, and even despair. After all, asking for things to happen for his own benefit is the way the non-Christian uses prayer too.

The Air Force chaplain meets a pilot walking across the tarmac. "Do you pray?" he asks.

"Yes, of course!"

"Well, I've never seen you at my chapel services."

"No, chaplain. I only pray when I'm flying—when I am on the ground I can cope."

Typically, the non-Christian uses prayer to get what he wants, what will make his life easy and happy. For many of us, God is almost like Aladdin's "genie of the lamp" to be called to do our bidding. "Master," the genie asks Aladdin, "What is *your* will?" But when the non-Christian doesn't get his request, he disposes of the genie. "I prayed for my son to come back from the war. He didn't. Now I now longer believe in God." "I prayed that my wife would be cured of cancer. When she wasn't, I gave up on God."

What if prayer doesn't work?

The Christian can easily adopt a similar attitude. What if his prayer does not get him what he wants? If Jerry does not land a new job; if Jackie fails her exams; if Jonathan remains single; if Jill finds no snow because of the mildest winter on record when she reaches Colorado; if Jean's gall bladder operation is not a success; if Jim breaks his car axle on a remote mountain road; if Joanie comes back from the used car lots without having found one car she could afford —what then?

Some Christians will tell you that the fault was in the way you prayed—as if God would only answer to one magic formula. On a European holiday we went to visit the cascade at Schaffhausen in Switzerland. At the German border we disposed of all our German money by buying gas because we were returning to England through France and would not need German currency again. Thirty minutes later we parked in one of the designated lots by the cascade. There were warning signs that only Swiss francs would operate the release gate to leave the lot. However, we had some coins left over from the previous year and so, when we left, we fed the coins into the machine. Out they fell again! The gate did not lift. We tried again, banging the machine. Still no result. By now quite a number of vehicles had lined up behind us. There were some vigorous comments in German. *They* tried the coins. Same result. Suddenly, to our deep embarrassment, one German noticed that we were using French francs! More embarrassment —the machine only worked with German marks or Swiss francs. We had disposed of all our German ones. We had not broken any Swiss notes. In the nick of time a friendly German paid for us, and the forty-car line-up burst out of the parking lot.

But God is not like that. He does not decline to respond if we don't put in the right prayer "coin." He is not a pagan God who, before he will answer, demands a particular incantation or a ritual of magical words or actions. He is our heavenly Father, dealing with us in love, as his children. Ours is a family relationship. So the problems encountered by Jerry, Jill and the others cannot be explained away simply by saying they didn't pray properly.

Results of prayer in the Bible

What about incidents in the Bible? Here again we see the same variety of prayers and answers to prayer that we observe in our own lives. Here are a few examples:

> The son of Paul's sister hears of an ambush to kill Paul. Paul avoids the ambush and lives (Acts 23), while Stephen is arrested, and after preaching, is stoned to death (Acts 7).

> Peter is miraculously delivered from prison by the angel of the Lord, while others pray for him (Acts 12), but John the Baptist is kept in prison, then beheaded, and his head brought in on a platter (Mark 6).

> The lame man at the temple is healed instantly by Peter, and walks and leaps (Acts 3), but Epaphroditus, a great

servant of God, has a long, nearly fatal, illness (Phil. 2:26).

A boy falls asleep during Paul's sermon, falls from the third floor and is taken up for dead. Paul raises him to life (Acts 20). But when Trophimus is ill, Paul has to leave him behind at Miletus (2 Tim. 4:20).

James affirms "The prayer of faith will save the sick" (James 5), but Timothy is instructed to take a little wine for his frequent stomach ailments (1 Tim. 5:23).

Jesus commands the storm on the lake to stop, and the boat comes safely to shore (Mark), but the storm on the Mediterranean is allowed to run its full course. The boat is wrecked, though all are saved (Acts 27).

Prayers answered and unanswered
We are aware of this variation in our lives and in the lives of those close to us. The telephone rings and we listen, incredulously, to the words, "I'm terribly sorry to tell you that Ruth has active, lymphoblastic leukemia." Ruth, one of our nieces, was then fifteen—a likeable Christian girl preparing to take her "O" level examinations. Leukemia! Just the sound of it makes the blood run cold. This young life with so much potential for Christ—and now leukemia. The disease had been spotted rapidly and diagnosed accurately. Ruth was immediately taken into a hospital. Was there any hope? I will mention some more details later in the book, but suffice it to say here that her family (who are Christians) prayed with unswerving faith; her home church began regular and realistic times of special prayer; we and many others prayed fervently. In God's mercy the treatment, the timing and other circumstances worked together. Ruth recovered completely, with her faith and witness radiant, seeming to want to live twice as fully for Jesus Christ as before. That was more than ten years ago. Ruth became a medical student at the hospital where she was treated and

married another medic. Dr. Ruth sees her life as given back to her by God.

Yes, we believe in God's healing in answer to prayer.

At about the same time, however, and in the same church, another young person became seriously ill, of similar age and faith, from a praying family and the same praying church. He too was carried to God on the stretcher of faith-prayer. But he died. "Why?" asked their beloved pastor, Andrew McKeill. In the same church, with the same love and prayer, why does one live and one die?

I was sitting at the back of the church during a special meeting. We were celebrating the long life and ministry of one of God's faithful saints who had been out on the mission field for a lifetime and was continuing his witness for Christ at home, still going strong at ninety. Then came news from Manorom Hospital in Thailand of a terrible car accident on the way to a picnic, in which several brilliant young surgeons, their wives and children—all in Thailand to serve Christ—were suddenly snatched from the world with a harshness that numbs one's heart. Why? Why such loss? Why such devastation to the work of God at Manorom? And why should some servants of God live on this earth into their nineties and others be taken so young?

Several college kids are searching for apartments at the start of a new school year. They pray. Suddenly one finds "the perfect place." He gives thanks in his prayer group and overflows with gratitude and joy. The others are downcast. They are still searching, still praying.

All these examples end up in problems *if* we start with ourselves as the center, not God. If God is there, only to do *our* bidding, then naturally we will discard him if he "doesn't work." Of course we would not put it as bluntly as that, but it is what we feel.

A girl asks to see me after a service. We sit down in a pew together. "What's wrong?" I ask.

"God doesn't keep his promises."

"What do you mean?"

"God doesn't keep his promises," she repeats.

I venture a direct approach: "What you mean, I think, is that you have asked God for a husband and yet you remain single." I am on target. Her view of God and prayer is "the genie of the lamp." "Ask what you will, believing, and you will receive it." She has asked for a husband. She has not received. No other possibilities or factors are allowed in this simplistic approach. God is to blame. He scores nil and is to be discarded.

Here is a married couple—happy and apparently Christian, involved in the life of the church. The wife contracts cancer. The husband is desperate. He asks for prayer, hears about faith healers and is prepared to try anything. The situation worsens. The cancer is rampant. There is special prayer with the laying on of hands. As the cancer advances further it would seem time to face up to the inevitable, to share what, for husband and wife, is left of life together. Instead, there is a frenetic insistence that God is going to heal. He *must* heal. How can he allow a beloved wife to suffer and die? When the wife dies, the reaction is sadly predictable. The husband turns away from God in bitterness and cuts himself off from the One who could surround him in love, thus also separating himself emotionally from his believing spouse, who is now with the Lord. Many people are hurt, all because the prayer of the man started from self requiring God to do *his* will.

We will never be able to sort out the privileges and problems of prayer when *we* are at the center.

So "let's start at the beginning"—God.

Re-focusing in prayer

We need a God-centered perspective. The world revolves around *God,* not around me. There are more than four billion people in the world and you and I are just two of them; we will only begin to see ourselves in perspective

when we realize we are only a tiny part of the human race
—a part of God's creation under his sovereign control.
There are millions of believing Christians in the world and
you and I are just two of them; we will only begin to understand ourselves as Christians when we see ourselves as a
small fraction of the Body of Christ.

We need a God-centered trust. If we walk around a vast
farming area in Iowa we may find it difficult to understand
why one field is cultivated, another lies fallow, another is
being used for hay. If I start with my limited understanding
of farming, I shall be puzzled. I must start instead with the
farmer. What is his overall purpose—why is growth occur-
ring in one field and nothing happening in another? He
knows. It is in his plan. I may not comprehend it, but if I
know the farmer and I can be confident that he knows
what he's doing, I must trust him.

So that is where we must start understanding prayer. We
must start with the Lord over all, the Creator, Sustainer,
the Head of the Body, the Lord of the Church, the Divine
Farmer, in whose world, body, church and harvest field we
find ourselves.

The person who *is* the Beginning—he's the only good
place to start.

CHAPTER 2

THE FIRST FOUNDATION: FAITH IN GOD AS GOD

IT IS ONE THING TO SAY "O.K. Prayer starts with God," but how do we work that out? How do we establish understanding and convictions that will stand the test of anything life throws at us in the future? There are five foundations to build. The first, which we will discuss in this chapter, is faith in God as God.

The faith foundation

Faith must lay hold of God, whatever the circumstances. It has to be learned when the sky is blue if it is to be proved when the clouds come. It was out of such long-established conviction that Paul could write to Timothy from prison: "I am not ashamed, because I know *whom* I have believed [in whom I have trusted], and am convinced that he is able to guard what I have entrusted to him for that day." (2 Tim.

1:12 NIV) It was not imprisonment that filled Paul's mind but the Lord and his absolute faithfulness. Similarly, on a ship in the middle of the raging storm in the Mediterranean, Paul was assured by God that all the passengers would be saved and so he could shout the words across the deck in the teeth of the wind: "I believe God that it will be exactly as I have been told."

So often the psalmist was bewildered by events that he could not explain. Suffering seemed to continue; the heathen prospered; he felt forsaken and a long way from God. Yet whenever he felt like this he fought back to the foundational conviction: "Who is a rock except our God?" (Ps. 18:31) and "though the earth trembles, the mountains shake and the waters roar, we will not fear" because "God is our refuge and strength, a very present help in trouble" (Ps. 46:1-2). In just the same way we often need to stop, put the brakes on, let the dust settle and get our perspective restored. Events overwhelm us, crashing in on us one after the other like the waves on the seashore. God wants us to pause, to be quiet. He says: "Be still, and know that I am God." We need to get our perspective restored day after day. He is God and we belong to him. Everything else is secondary to that wonderful fact. We must let it grip us, flood our hearts. We can leap down the street in its joy. The Lord is God. The Lord is *God*! And we belong to Him for ever!

This is what grips the heart of Habakkuk and shines through his amazing words of testimony: "Though the fig tree does not blossom, nor fruit be on the vines, the produce of the olive fail, and the fields yield no food, the flock be cut off from the fold and there be no herd in the stalls, yet I will rejoice in the Lord!" (Hab. 3:17).

To the city dwellers, the cutting force of that testimony is blunted. To feel its force we must relocate it in a modern city. "Though my business schemes fail, profits turn to losses, I lose my job, my bank balance dwindles to nothing, and I cannot see where I am going to get another job or support my family, yet I will rejoice in the Lord!" He trusts God, even when the picture is utterly bleak. Can I do that? Could I have done that in the face of torture and murder in Cambodia? Could I do that in the waterless deserts around the Red Sea where drought seems perpetual? Am I, in my present circumstances, able to focus on God every time and to trust him, even when I do not understand all the events that are happening to me?

God's honor roll of faith in Hebrews 11 hit me vividly a few years ago. Until then I had not seen the full orbit of walking by faith. The phrase "The just shall live by faith" (or "my righteous one shall live by faith") had represented to me the battle-cry of salvation, of being right with God through faith alone. But in Hebrews 10:38 I discovered that it refers to the continuing Christian life as well. No longer could I feel that faith was a milestone passed long ago when I came to Christ as my Savior. It was now to challenge my thinking, daring, acting and pioneering for Christ —not just receiving Christ and then living life as comfortably as possible but receiving Christ and continuing with him at the center. Hebrews 11 presents four categories of faith worked out in practice, faith without which "it is impossible to please him" (Heb. 11:6).

Worthship faith This is faith that puts God at the center of our lives because he is worthy of all our honor and adoration. We come to realize that he is worth more to us than any human, than any thing or being in the whole universe. Abel expresses this with simple profundity when he and Cain bring offerings to God. Cain brings "of the fruit of the ground" but Abel brings "of the firstlings of his flock and of their fat portions." We can imagine Cain going out of his garden and picking a few things at random so that he has something to offer. But Abel chooses his best—the firstlings of the flock and the fat portions. For him only the choicest is good enough for God. His giving reflects his "worthship faith."

Almost nothing sorts out our Christian integrity and love for the Lord as quickly as giving. How do we give on a Sunday? Are we like Cain, delving into our pockets as the collection plate is passed, giving something, but without much thought or sacrifice, giving because it looks bad not to? Or are we like Abel—loving God, eager to see his work go forward, expressing this in thought, through planned, proportionate giving and in overflowing love-gifts as well. Of course, giving is not confined to a Sunday nor to "Christian" projects, but our giving is a reliable indicator of whether we have God "at the center."

Exploit faith Hebrews 11 is full of examples of what we might call "exploit faith." It is exciting to recall the great faith of men like Noah, Abraham, and Moses. They dared and obeyed. They witnessed the floods of judgment, the making of a nation, the deliverance from Egypt, the crossing of the Red Sea, and much more. Our blood is fired as we read of what happened. Even the film-makers have been fascinated and have produced their biblical epics.

Applying the lessons of "exploit faith" is also exciting in our own time. The God of the patriarchs is our God today, the leader of his twentieth century people into further adventures of faith that result in exciting provision, growth, and spiritual power. I'm an enthusiastic "exploit" man, as I have described in *The Moses Principle* (Harold Shaw Publishers, 1978), and since writing that book, I have had the joy of seeing countless ventures elsewhere proving God to be the same God. Exploits for God, when God calls and man obeys, are a further indicator that God is at the center.

Deliverance faith Then in Hebrews 11:33-35 we are introduced to that element of faith by which special events are possible, as when people have been supernaturally . strengthened for battle, or when the mouths of lions have been stopped, in Daniel's case. Even resurrection from the dead is mentioned here. How exciting it is to see such things happen! What joy we feel when a friend is suddenly healed, or someone is released from a communist prison-camp, or a visa is granted for a missionary at the last minute, after months of waiting. Such matters are the theme of the church's prayer-gathering, or of sharing with other friends in prayer, and we all gather to praise God together when deliverance happens in answer to faith. There are endless paperback books telling stories of deliverance faith, and they are avidly consumed. We expect God to be supernaturally involved in our daily lives and so "deliverance faith" is a third indicator that we have "God at the center."

Crisis faith There is another category of faith described in Hebrews 11—a category that is often omitted. Here, in verse 36, are individuals who suffered mocking, scourging, chains, imprisonment. They were stoned, sawn in two, killed with the sword; they went about in skins of sheep and goats, destitute, afflicted, ill-treated, by *faith*? Yes, by faith! They had no exploit to recall years later; no deliverance to give praise for in the prayer gathering. Instead, persecution to death, suffering and torture—what the world would call "disaster." Those who would want us to believe that if we have enough faith we can be healed or delivered from anything never mention those who did *not* triumph. But here in Hebrews 11 we have faith at its highest—faith that holds onto the living God when there is no light in the darkness, no relief from the agony and no remission of the pain and disease. When men and women go on believing in the Lord in spite of such circumstances, their faith is faith indeed! Millions have demonstrated such faith—those who have been murdered simply for professing Christ, those who have spent long years in Siberian labor camps because they spoke up for Christ and truth, those who have been incarcerated in the body-packed cells of death camps under some insanely evil regime. Yet they believed as did their Savior before them on the cross. They believed in God. There is no doubt at all that they had "God at the center."

If we are to understand prayer we must start by building this first foundation—the foundation of the centrality of God in our lives. Our faith—worthship faith, exploit faith, deliverance faith, crisis faith—must hold onto him whatever happens, even when we cannot understand or explain it. It is of such faith that William Barclay said: "Obstacles will not daunt it, delays will not depress it, discouragement will not take its hope away."

CHAPTER 3

THE SECOND FOUNDATION: THE CHARACTER OF GOD

THE SECOND FOUNDATION TO BE BUILT into our lives before we can approach the question of prayer is the character of God. We have already said that faith must hold onto God even when it does not understand what is happening. But we are more likely to "hang in there"—hold on—when we know something about the God onto whom we are holding. We will also learn when not to hang in there, when repentance must precede petition, when correction of life is a prerequisite for God to hear our prayers.

A God who winks at sin?
When you think about it, it is amazing that people can live in total disregard of God—disobeying his laws, not bothering to follow him—yet blithely expecting his help as soon as trouble comes. God is hardly personal to them. They view

him more as a distant prayer-receiver to be switched "on" or "off," and they may even select which religious or denominational channel to use! How far that is from the reality of prayer, in its close, constant, personal relationship with the Lord and in its atmosphere of love, trust, and obedience.

Yet even Christians often devalue the character of God in prayer. One Sunday morning after the service was over, a committed Christian young woman asked to see me. She was obviously upset. "I have been praying for an answer all week and haven't received one," she blurted out. The matter was clearly urgent, so I asked her to explain. Her sister had just had a baby in Canada and she wanted to go and visit her. In just a few months her time in England would be over and she would be returning permanently to Canada, but she wanted to make this quick trip now. A friend of hers had just flown over from Canada on a cheap round-trip ticket but did not intend to return. (At the time it was cheaper to get a round trip than a one-way ticket!) So here was the chance to use her friend's ticket. Then she could get a cheap one-way ticket herself for her last few months back in England. Of course, it meant assuming her friend's identity and borrowing her passport, but they looked alike. She had been praying about this all week, and God had not answered! Because of her deep desire to see her sister and the baby it took some time to help her to understand that you cannot plan something contrary to the character of God and expect him to fit in with your purpose. Between us, we resolved that she would approach the airline to see if there was any legal way of transferring the ticket. There wasn't. She did not go. But she learned a lesson for a lifetime; that prayer cannot be effective unless it is aligned with the character of God, who is uncompromisingly righteous.

Here are an attractive Christian young man and woman. They have a guidance problem and have come to me for advice. Though both are involved in leadership responsibilities within the church, I discover in our conversation that they are sleeping together, though unmarried. They think nothing of it because "everybody's doing it." I attempt to show them how deeply God values the beauty and exclusiveness of the sexual relationship, and that it is the climax of commitment, not a cheap forerunner. But particularly, in the light of their need for guidance, I try to show them that they cannot sin deliberately and consciously against God's law and at the same time expect divine guidance and answers to prayer. God is not a machine. He is personal. His character has been shown to us. He is holy.

The cause of the collapse of Samaria and the fall of Jerusalem in Old Testament history was not mightier armies from outside, but moral collapse from within. The Lord told his people how he hated their feasts and their acts of worship because their lives were full of cruelty, lust, oppression of the poor, and self-centeredness that sickened his heart. God's attitude toward such hypocrisy is there in black and white for us to see and understand. We cannot expect God to answer our prayers if we are deliberately living outside the bounds of love and obedience to him. The reason for unanswered prayer too often lies in *us*.

The love-promise of God

Many other aspects of the character of God will challenge, strengthen, or enrich our praying, but none so much as the covenant love of God. The great Hebrew word *hesed* is the anchor word of the Old Testament. Translated variously as "mercy" or "steadfast love," it is *the* word to which the believer is to cling, the word by which he moves through the thickest jungle of despair, the word to which he climbs from the lowest depths of depression.

Israel had been conceived and born in God's covenant love. As the solemn promises were made and the blood shed, God took these people as *his* people, as his beloved, and even though Israel and Judah presumed on that covenant love—taking it for granted, often ignoring its moral demands—the love itself never altered. That God pleaded for a heart-response to his covenant love, not just a series of meaningless ritual sacrifices, is vividly demonstrated in Hosea 6:6 and throughout the startling "living parable" of the whole book of Hosea. So when the nation fell into the hands of the invaders and the people were carried off despairing, into captivity, their prophets focused on the only rock of hope that remained unmoved: the covenant love of God. Sinking in the bog of misery and shame, the expatriate Israelites could still lay hold of the unshakable truth: "The steadfast love of the Lord never ceases, his mercies never come to an end; they are new every morning; great is thy faithfulness" (Lam. 3:22-23).

Making the covenant personal
In the New Testament, the picture of a "new covenant" began to emerge, coming to its glorious fruition in the cross of Jesus Christ. When Jesus himself took the bread and wine, symbols of his body and blood, at the Last Supper, he said: "This is the new covenant in my blood." It is into this eternal covenant of love that we, today, may enter by faith in Christ, and it is on the immovable rock of that covenant love that we must set our feet. The Holy Spirit moves us from a mere mental acceptance into a joyful inward experience. God's love (that is, the understanding of God's love for us in Christ) "has been poured into our hearts through the Holy Spirit which has been given to us" (Rom. 5:5), and the sense of that love is part of the "honeymoon experience" when we first come into personal Christian faith —especially when that experience is clear and decisive rather than gradual. How often a new believer wants literally to leap for joy at the wonder of it all and the overflowing sense of the love of the Lord. One of the most popular jobs in the church to which I belong is the care of those who have just come to faith in Christ—popular, be-

cause week by week older Christians work alongside people in the first wonder of the covenant love of God. For so many new-found faith is a "pouring into the heart" or "flooding of the heart" with God's love by the Holy Spirit.

After the honeymoon

Yet as we go on in the Christian life we do not live in a constant honeymoon, even though we often revel in the special touches of his love along the way. Instead, we go deeper into the effect of that covenant love on the whole of living. So Romans 5 moves on to Romans 8. Here we are reminded of the realities of life in a sinful world—trouble, hardship, persecution, famine, destitution, danger, or "sword." If we expect prayer to bring us a trouble-free life we shall be disillusioned. Here there is no promise of escape, or of freedom from trial and pain. Instead, we are promised that none of these things—*none* of them—can separate us from the love of Christ. This is the key to triumphant living as a Christian—a confidence in the unchanging love that holds us, always.

This does not mean that we do not pray. We will pray when sickness strikes or when there is financial hardship or when we cannot find a job or must cope as a widow with young children. We will pray when we are being ridiculed as Christians, or imprisoned, or sent to a labor-camp. We will pray in the face of danger, in time of war, in the midst of accident or disaster. Sometimes we will give thanks for our Lord's evident intervention; other times we will not see it that way. In this sinful, fallen world Christians get caught in the middle of war, epidemics, or earthquakes like anybody else; they are as prone to cardiac arrest or cancer as agnostics or atheists. But the supreme, over-riding factor for the Christian in any and every experience of life is that nothing—no powers or force, no nuclear war or global holocaust, not even death itself—can separate us from the love of God in Christ Jesus our Lord. We must build this foundation securely so that when troubles or problems come, we are not shaken and our faith stands firm.

Henry Venn—a great Christian who lived 200 years ago had to bear the death of his wife, leaving him with five young children. He wrote: "Did I not know the Lord to be mine, were I not certain his heart feels even more love for me than I am able to conceive, were not this evident to me, not by deduction and argument, but by consciousness, by his own light shining in my soul as the sun does upon my bodily eyes, into what a deplorable condition should I have been now cast?"

Henry Venn was able to grasp the immovable rock of God's love, but not everybody feels the love of God as he did in that devastating time of his life. Others lose all sense of the love of God—they feel cold and prayer seems impossible. Yet for them too the only path of restoration will be by means of the same rock of covenant love.

When I was working in Manchester I learned a lesson about this from Mary Hollinshead, our church worker. An elderly member of the congregation—a lovely Christian woman, full of good works, one who cared for others and served the Lord with joy and faithfulness—had entered the hospital with cancer. She was the last person you would expect to lose her faith, but that is what happened. Mary went to visit her and rapidly summed up the situation. "I am not going to leave your bedside," she said, "until I hear you say again, from your heart, 'God is love,'" It seemed tough treatment! Mary read to her from the Scriptures, talked with her, prayed with her. Eventually the elderly lady said with conviction, "My God is love." Later, when she left the hospital for a while she told the whole church: "That was the turning point." I have often followed Mary's example in ministering to others and am thankful for being shown the need to concentrate on that one foundation.

Faith in context
The character of God should be much in our minds as we

pray, whether the sun is shining or the clouds are heavy. We will be encouraged in our whole approach to our Lord as we contemplate his wisdom, love, righteousness, goodness. George Müller, founder of an orphanage in Bristol in the nineteenth century, demonstrated a faith that God honored in exciting and very practical ways. Many are the stories of food delivered "at the last minute" or the exact sum of money required arriving in the morning mail, but it is also important to see the context of his faith. As he writes in his journal of a moment when they were down to the last forty dollars and 100 people needed to be fed, he does not begin by asking God for the money or food, but tells us instead: "I was meditating on God's unchangeable love, power and wisdom, and turning all as I went to prayer." (For a deeper insight into the life of prayer and faith, read Roger Steer's biography, *George Müller: Delighted in God,* [Harold Shaw Publishers, 1975].)

God's loving character, then, is the second foundation to be firmly built on as we approach the subject of prayer. The onslaught of doubts such as "Why should this happen to me? Why do I have to endure this suffering? Why doesn't God answer my prayer? Why doesn't God do what I ask?" will still come, but it will be met by an unshakable conviction, an immovable foundation. Though I may not be able to explain why God does or does not seem to answer; though I feel only emptiness and desolation; yet I know God is love, that I am united to him forever by his covenant and that nothing can separate me from that eternal love.

CHAPTER 4

THE THIRD FOUNDATION: THE PURPOSES OF GOD

THE THIRD PRAYER FOUNDATION TO BE BUILT concerns who is in control. The popular, secular concept of prayer has ourselves "in control," with God "out there" to do our bidding when called upon. He is seen as available to help us get what we want. We have our plans, our hopes, our purposes and God is expected to fit in with them. If he doesn't, then we don't bother to pray anymore.

God, a convenience
The seeds of this approach are often sown in childhood. "Now children, we are having our picnic on Saturday, so let's pray that God will give us a sunny day." The children pray in faith. "It will be sunny on Saturday, Mommy, because we asked God for a sunny day." "What wonderful faith the children have," say the adults to one another. But

what do they mean by "faith"? Isn't it a faith in a God who is there to do our will?

On Saturday the day dawns with a blue sky. It is a beautiful sunny day and, apart from some sunburn, the whole outing is delightful. "We prayed. God has given us this sunny day. Now let us thank God." The incident is over. Similar incidents will occur and if things do not work out as prayed for—if we get rain instead of sun, failure instead of success—it will be explained away with "the farmers needed rain." However, because the prayers originally prayed did not take that possibility into account the children will see prayer as manipulating God to do their wishes. As life goes on, this view of prayer inevitably begins to get shaken.

The loss of "faith"
I was sitting in a funeral car on the way to the cemetery. I had been ordained only a few weeks and I was new to reactions to death in that city parish. It was a tragic situation —the sudden death of a child.

"It makes you wonder," sighed the grandmother.

"What do you mean?" I asked in my naivete.

"Whether there's a God at all," she responded. Here was the "God-is-not-doing-what-we-asked" attitude. Later in my ministry I became accustomed to such remarks. Often they are accompanied by the admission "I've lost my faith." "I prayed for my husband to come back safe from the war and he was killed .... I've lost my faith." "I prayed for my child to be protected every day and yet she had that accident on her bicycle.... I've lost my faith." Gently one has to point out, "That sort of 'faith' needs to be lost. It isn't Christian faith."

Yet how far do we let that sort of thinking creep into our praying even as Christians?

First things first
We need deliberately and constantly to re-affirm as Chris-

tians that the purposes of God are greater and more important than the purposes of man. In becoming a Christian "by one Spirit we were all baptized into one body" (1 Cor. 12:13). Our function as members of the body of Christ is to fulfill the purposes of the Head. Our roles will vary, but together with the other members, we acknowledge with our lives that Christ is our Lord. Our greatest task and privilege in life is to fulfill his purposes for us and through us. Once this vision has filled our hearts and minds, our own purposes, wants, and needs become secondary.

Jesus expressed this principle in his Sermon on the Mount. "Do not worry about your life, what you will eat or drink; or about your body, what you will wear. Is not life more important than food, and the body more important than clothes? . . . For the pagans run after all these things, and your heavenly Father knows that you need them. But seek *first* his kingdom and his righteousness, and all these things will be given to you as well" (Matt. 6:25-33 NIV).

It isn't that our heavenly Father is unconcerned about the practical things—his care is that of a Father. But the purposes of his kingdom are more urgent and they must become more important to us in our praying and living. Thus, our prayer requests must be submitted to the over-riding purposes of our God, who sees the end from the beginning.

Let's see the same principle in a human setting. As a family we have been in Switzerland on vacation, camping in our van and revelling in the wonderful scenery. Now we are driving back through France. It is around noon and we are all hungry. Ahead of us is a place where we could pull the car off the road under the shade of trees next to a beautiful meadow and stream. "Just the place for a picnic, Dad, let's stop." Now imagine my answer: a warm "Sure. Great idea!" as I steer the van over to the selected spot. Certainly as a father I would be delighted for us all to enjoy the picnic together in that lovely place. So if I can, I will say "Yes." But I may have to say "No," in spite of the chorus of dismay

from the back of the car. I won't enjoy saying "No." Nor will
I enjoy the thought of everyone getting hungrier (although
some fruit distributed around the car may help for a while).
My "No" will only be because of a more important purpose
—catching the channel ferry at Calais.

God's time frame

So often when we pray to our heavenly Father about something affecting our lives or the lives of others, the Father
says, "Yes, of course, let's enjoy this together." We rejoice in
the answer to prayer, and in the sense of his presence and
blessing. Yet there will be the times when some greater purpose has to be the deciding factor and when our request
must be put on one side or its answer delayed.

Zechariah and Elizabeth learned this lesson in Luke 1.
Their longing for a child must often have been on their lips
in prayer. There seems to have been nothing in them to
prevent their prayer being answered; they "were both
righteous before God, walking in all the commandments
and ordinances of the Lord blameless." The explanation
for the delay was that God had chosen Elizabeth to bear
John the Baptist as a son. As a herald of the appearance of
Christ, the timing of John's birth was all-important. He was
a vital part of the greater purposes of the Lord.

My "good" or God's best?

It seems, too, that at different points in our lives or in the
development of a church or Christian work, God may alter
his ways of answering prayer in order to train us, mature
us or help us concentrate on different aspects of his work.
He did this in the ministry of Jesus. Healing miracles
abounded, signs of who he was up to the acclamation "You
are the Christ." Then they become very rare. Jesus turns
his attention to teaching the disciples and is far less involved
in public preaching and healing.

People today who expect specific miracles to happen all

the time to demonstrate the power of God may have over-looked this changing pattern in the Gospels. The Lord has his purposes and if we really want to follow him we will be sensitive to his leading and to his changes of emphasis in our lives and work. It is the same with his gifts to us. They are to enable us to serve and it seems likely that in some people some gifts will be temporary and in others they will last for life, as it suits the Head of the body. The lesson in our lives and in our churches is that we may not decide God's purposes in advance or assume that what he pur-posed to do through a sequence of events ten years ago he will repeat through a similar sequence today. Prayer seeks and submits to God's changing purposes as they are worked out for the welfare of the church.

When I was first ordained I was heavily involved in work among youth and children. In this context I planned to take a lively bunch of 10- to 12-year-olds away for a holiday, renting a converted railway car situated at the end of a quiet branch line by the sea. I was particularly pleased with the arrangements and when they were finally clinched by tele-phone I raced through to the kitchen to tell my wife, jumped in the air for joy and more-or-less knocked myself out by hitting the doorpost with my head! However, I was to receive a second blow. My vicar said, "You can't take them there. You can't have these boys staying near a train track, it's too dangerous." I was annoyed, disappointed, hurt, and generally frustrated! However, the result was that I took them instead to a superb camp run by a national Christian organization. What the boys received was so much better in every way than what I could have done for them, and it began an association with that camp that lasted for many years to come. The vicar's "old-fashioned ideas" turned out to be a part of the Lord's greater purposes.

Is this not also true in the delicate matter of singleness and marriage? I think of some of my friends in the ministry who are single, who could never fulfill the important ministry

to which they have been called if they were married. Because of constant, worldwide travel, or special Christian
attributes, skills, or insights which demand much time for
development for the benefit of the wider church, their
singleness is an asset. They are free to give all their time to
God and his work. On the other hand, there are ministries
of Christian leadership that would lose a great deal if they
were not led by married people. Mine is one of them! Of
course, the decision is not as clear as that for many, but
where individuals have accepted singleness positively and
committed themselves and their singleness to the Lord's
purposes, it has usually strengthened their character and
made them effective fellow-workers for Christ.

Sometimes we have too narrow a vision to understand
the purposes of God. When I was in my late teens, prior to
being drafted by the Army, I was a sea cadet. I spent a week
at "camp" in Londonderry, Northern Ireland. One day we
went out on a destroyer for submarine-hunting in the Irish
Sea. It was rather like a sophisticated, marine version of
cops and robbers. There were several destroyers involved
in the "games." We began by dropping buoys into the Irish
Sea over a wide area. Attached to these buoys were radio
transmitters. The destroyers would sound to the sea-bed
far below them, listening for echoes of the submarines in
their area, but that was all they could do, apart from
keeping tuned in to a plane overhead. Only the plane had
the receiving equipment to hear from all those little trans-
mitting buoys. When the plane eventually heard a sub-
marine's echo it gave the position and the first destroyer
to reach the spot was the winner. I can still remember the
feeling of comparative helplessness on the destroyer, able
to see only a small segment of the ocean, totally dependent
on the plane above that could see the whole picture. That
has been the imagery of guidance for me ever since. I may
discern correctly the town, church, office contacts, and
needs around me, but they're only one small part of the

Lord's vast universe. He can see it all—the needs in India, Africa or the United States as well. He can see inside the walls of Russian prisons or New York skyscrapers or English suburban houses. He knows us through and through, with all our strengths, talents, and flaws. No one else can more accurately fit me into God's purposes than God himself!

As William Cowper put it:

Deep in unfathomable mines
Of never-failing skill,
He treasures up His bright designs
And works His sovereign will.

His purposes will ripen fast
Unfolding every hour;
The bud may have a bitter taste
But sweet will be the flower.

Blind unbelief is sure to err
And scan His work in vain;
God is his own interpreter
And He will make it plain.

Of course, as Cowper well knew, we do not always understand—at least, not at first. Peter, weeping his heart out at his denial of Jesus, was not likely to understand that Jesus had permitted his denial because out of the ashes of failure would rise a Peter full of new humility and power, who would write later to his fellow-Christians: "Humble yourselves therefore under the mighty hand of God, that in due time he may exalt you" (1 Pet. 5:6).

Job had to learn his lesson the hard way. We sympathize with all he suffered, but then he starts to dispute with God, basing his arguments on his own fixed ideas about sin and suffering. Suddenly the shoe is on the other foot. No longer is it Job questioning God but God questioning Job: "Where were you when I laid the foundations of the earth?" Finally

Job gets things straight: "I know that you can do all things, and that no purpose of yours can be thwarted. I have uttered what I did not understand, things too wonderful for me, which I did not know...." There was so much more than Job could ever have understood because it was beyond the human scene—Satan being unleashed to test him.

The broad dimensions of the spiritual battle, of the wrestling with huge principalities and powers, of the global plans and purposes of our Lord, makes us marvel that we have a part to play at all! But we have, as members of his body. So, though we may often wish we could have the curtain lifted occasionally, as it was for Elisha's servant, and see that "those who are with us are more than those who are with them" (2 Kings 6:16), we must be prepared to accept his purposes by faith. He will not be thwarted. He is "working his purpose out as year succeeds to year."

Here, then, is the third foundation to lay if we are to understand prayer. We must accept gladly the fact that much as our heavenly Father encourages us to bring everything to him in prayer, and much as he loves to answer and bless, we are to seek first his kingdom—and make his purposes primary in our lives.

CHAPTER 5

THE FOURTH FOUNDATION: THE WAYS OF GOD

THE FOURTH FOUNDATION FOR EFFECTIVE PRAYER is that of openness to the ways of the Lord.

Within our human families we often assume that our way of doing things is the norm for everyone and we are surprised to find that other families have different standards. In eating, for example, others may be more informal than we are, or more formal, with an evening meal at a set time, when everyone changes for dinner. When we visit other countries we often find even more striking differences. The Britisher, using his knife and fork together seems odd to the American. The American habit of cutting food up with the knife, then laying it down and picking up the fork to eat with seems odd to the Britisher. Once, when I was in a high-class restaurant in Los Angeles, the waiter came round to ask whether I wanted a "doggie-bag" for left-overs. I couldn't believe it!

A German Christian young woman came to England as an "au pair" (exchange domestic worker). The Christian family with whom she lived was shocked when she announced one Sunday afternoon that she was going out to see a movie. "But we don't *do* that on Sunday," demurred her hostess. Later in the afternoon the girl saw her hostess knitting. Now she was shocked! "But we don't do *that* on Sunday in Germany." They both laughed at the incongruity of the situation. How often we label things "right" or "wrong" in accordance with our own way of living.

Our way—or God's?
We can do exactly the same with God about his ways of answering prayer. As we pray for something we often have a mental picture of how God could—or should!—answer. When I was facing up to God's call to the ministry I knew that there was to be a special weekend conference at our church dealing with the problems of vocation and ministry, in early January. I had already been wakened to the call and had been praying for confirmation. This, I resolved, was to be the weekend that God would make his way clear. I went to all the meetings expectantly, but at the end of the Sunday evening nothing had happened. I was no further forward. There had been no clear "word from the Lord." Then, around midnight when I opened a book of devotional readings and turned to the portion for the day, I was startled to see that the text was from Isaiah 6: "Whom shall I send and who will go for us?" And the commentary on the text was as electric as a live wire for me. Every sentence, every word, was for me and made complete sense. I felt overwhelmed by the presence of the Lord and dropped to my knees with Isaiah's words on my lips, "Lord, here am I, send me." His ways, his timing were completely different from mine.

That is our God. He told us so:

"My thoughts are not your thoughts
Neither are your ways my ways, says the Lord.
For as the heavens are higher than the earth
So are my ways higher than your ways
And my thoughts than your thoughts." (Isa. 55:8)

That is how God acted in Old Testament history—supernaturally he delivered his people from slavery, provided their food in the wilderness, chose as king the shepherd-boy David, taught his people in exile, and restored them to Jerusalem. All these acts and many more bore the distinct stamp of God at work, in his own way.

But none of these events was as surprising to the human race as his way of making our salvation possible. Who would have thought of the Incarnation, the humble birth in a stable, the simple life-style of a carpenter, the death on the cross, the resurrection, the gift of the Holy Spirit? That is our God. His ways are "extra-ordinary." They go far beyond our thought or expectation.

Our minds need constantly to re-learn this truth. We must not confine God's ways of answering prayer to what we expect or to what we think he can manage.

The God of the unexpected

It was our God who raised up a heathen king, Cyrus, as his agent, even calling Cyrus his "shepherd" and his "anointed one." It was our God who did not preach a sermon at Elijah in the depths of spiritual depression in the desert, but delivered him a cake baked on hot stones and a jar of water. It was our God who spoke to the same Elijah, not in the dramatic denouement of the victory over pagan priests on Mount Carmel, not in the storm, earthquake, or wind that seemed to fit Elijah's own character, but in a still small voice. It was our God who chose to answer the Roman Cornelius's prayer by dealing with the Jewish Peter about his view of the Gentiles and then by the repetition of Pentecost—a pouring out of the Holy Spirit just as it had happened to the apostles "at the beginning." It was our God who answered the urgent, earnest prayer of the church for Peter in prison by freeing him in a miraculous way, so that not even those who were praying could believe it! It was our God who blinded the great Saul on the Damascus road and used a "nobody"—Ananias—to be his messenger and agent to bring Saul into God's kingdom. It was our God who blocked Paul's plans all across Asia Minor until he ended up in Troas and was then called, surprisingly, to Macedonia and Europe. When God's people pray God's answers are often a complete surprise!

Down through the centuries of Christian history hundreds of thousands of such incidents have taken place. In every generation the Lord has answered prayer in his own way. If I picked but one example it would be the lovely story of Billy Bray, the Cornish evangelist of the early nineteenth century, who needed a pulpit for a chapel he was building. Seeing an old three-cornered cupboard at an auction sale he "knew it was the very thing" for making into a pulpit. He had no money, of course! However, an inquiry as to what it might be sold for provided not only the estimate of "six shillings" but the actual cash from the person he asked. Billy was all set to bid "six shillings," but when the time came he was stunned to find himself outbid by a farmer. Surely God had meant him to have it. He decided to follow the "pulpit" on its journey to the farmer's house. There he witnessed the farmer's frustrated anger when he found that the cupboard would not fit through the door of the house. Faced with having to chop it up for firewood, the farmer was only too glad to accept Billy's offer of six shillings "if the farmer would have the cupboard transported to the chapel." Billy Bray was overjoyed. His heavenly Father had not only supplied the pulpit but had arranged for it to be delivered as well, all for six shillings!

Earlier, I mentioned my niece Ruth. Soon after her

leukemia was diagnosed my wife and I went to pray with her parents. It had been difficult to fix a time for us all to meet but suddenly it was possible and we asked a friend to come in as child-sitter. After she had arrived and as we began to leave she asked us what was wrong with Ruth. We told her. She responded at once, eagerly, "But I work for the top specialist in leukemia in the country; I am sure he would help." (We had not known this when we asked her to stay with our children). He was indeed willing to help, but only on the invitation of the specialist already dealing with Ruth. It turned out that the specialist knew the great man personally and was more than happy to have his help. So he kindly made the journey and saw Ruth several times. His expert knowledge was a significant help in commending, suggesting, and supporting the medical treatment. Mercifully, Ruth's leukemia went into remission. God's ways are higher than our ways.

At one time my wife, Myrtle, felt clearly called to missionary service but suddenly in an evening church meeting God "closed the door." Had she been wrong in her earlier sense of a call? Then she and I met. We fell in love and married into the ministry. God's earlier call had prepared the way and Myrtle had been willing to do anything and go anywhere for him, a very necessary preparation for life in the ministry. He called us both independently. God's ways are higher than our ways.

We may often learn from other Christians and other churches who have faced similar problems and challenges to ours. Principles of faith and prayer will often be the same —but God's ways of answering and working things out may be vastly different. Numbers of churches have tackled building projects and have adopted many of the faith principles described in *The Moses Principle*. Sometimes, seeing the challenges they have had to face, I have trembled. Yet when God calls his people out of Egypt he will faithfully bring them through the impossible into their Promised

Land. It has been wonderful to watch so many faith projects and see God dealing with each of them in his own way. God does not fit easily into books of methodology! His ways are higher than our ways.

So in prayer we learn to say "Lord, *your* will be done." It amazes me that some people will tell you that it shows lack of faith to tag "if it be your will" onto a prayer. On the contrary, it is a mark of true faith, because a vital part of faith is submission to the Lord and to his purposes and his ways. What we want most is his will, not ours. Let us not fall into the temptation of trying to persuade him to do *our* will!

This fourth prayer-foundation needs to be thoroughly and firmly laid. With Moses, let us cry from the heart, "Show me your ways." Just as "he made known his ways to Moses" (Ps. 103:7), let us wait on him to make his ways known to us. Let us trust him to work as he sees best.

CHAPTER 6

THE FIFTH FOUNDATION: THE PROMISES OF GOD

THE FIFTH PRAYER-FOUNDATION—the promises of God —is perhaps best thought of as a platform or floor, resting upon the four foundations we have already considered. Our motivation to come to God in prayer is because he has *invited* us to do so. He has reinforced that invitation with special promises about his willingness and readiness to hear and to answer. However, if we start with isolated promises as the foundation for prayer we get into difficulties.

How *not* to claim God's promises
Take John 15:7 for instance: "If you abide in me and my words abide in you, ask whatever you will and it shall be done for you." Peter is 17, facing ACT and SAT exams at school. He is a Christian. He takes hold of this promise "Ask whatever you will and it shall be done for you," and prays

for a composite score in the 98th percentile. Is he right or wrong? Angela longs for a steady boy friend, and then for marriage. She takes hold of this promise—and asks expectantly. Is she right or wrong? Scott is a children's evangelist. He prepares to speak at a youth rally. He takes hold of this promise and asks for seven conversions at the meeting. Is he right or wrong?

Another promise is in Mark 11:23-24: "Whoever says to this mountain, 'Be taken up and cast into the sea,' and does not doubt in his heart, but believes that what he says will come to pass, it will be done for him." Patricia has a problem with asthma. It makes life difficult for her and some of the attacks she gets, fighting for breath, are quite terrifying. Someone points her to this promise in Mark 11. She prays and claims the promise. Her asthma continues. She goes on praying and claiming the promise, without results. The person who showed her the verse tells her of someone who was fully delivered from asthma by claiming this promise, and goes on to suggest that Patricia doesn't have enough faith. She must exercise more faith and when her faith is strong enough the "mountain" of asthma will go. Patricia feels like a spiritual failure because she still has asthma. Or is the promise of God not reliable?

The promise platform
These "problems" arise only if we *start* with the promises. But when we stand on them as a platform already supported by the foundations of faith in God as God, the character of God, the purposes of God, and the ways of God, then the problems recede and the blessings are received.

Take the John 15 promise again. The context ("If you abide in me . . .") is of deep union with the Lord, as the branch in the vine. The whole focus is on the *centrality of God* (He is the vine, we are the branches), *the character of God* (his judgment, verses 2, 6; his cleansing, verse 3; and his love, verses 9-10), *the purposes of God* (to make us bearers of much fruit, verses 2, 4-5, 8; and for the Father thus to be glorified in us, verse 8) and *the ways of God* (removing dead branches, verses 2, 6; and pruning fruitful branches to produce more fruit, verse 2). The result in the Christian will be joy at being fruitfully used by the Lord. So, using John 15:7 as the basis for getting good exam scores, a husband, or a specific number of converts sounds oddly out of tune with the thrust of the whole chapter. Clearly the person who really wants to tune into the chapter will be praying for ways to glorify the Lord more and to be more fruitful in his service. This inevitably means pruning, and pruning hurts while it is happening, even if we can look back later and see reasons for it.

To press the point more sharply, if we really pray from the heart in terms of John 15:7 then we are openly saying to the Lord "You choose what way I can glorify you." It may be his will to glorify himself through strengthening us to triumph in and over a lifetime's affliction, as so clearly and marvellously demonstrated in the life of Joni Eareckson. Think of testimonies you have heard and Christian lives you have seen. Some have been snatched from disaster and others have shone in the midst of pain. This is the Hebrews 11 pattern we saw earlier. With the four foundations upholding it, John 15:7 will not be misused but will be a promise that we can dare to claim. Dare? Yes! Because we will be wanting God's glory and fruit in our lives above everything else. The similar promise in Mark 11:22-24 must be read in its context which also includes the four foundations of faith.

The disciples do not understand about the withered fig tree and its relationship to the disobedient and fruitless Jewish nation. It is beyond them, but Jesus brings them back to trust in God even when they do not understand. The character of God comes into the picture during Jesus' rebuke of the commercialization of the temple—the turning of God's "house of prayer" into a "den of robbers."

Later too, just after the promise, comes the reminder that we must approach prayer with an attitude of forgiveness to others so that we ourselves may be cleansed and forgiven. The closer we come to the promise of verses 23 and 24, the more we see that it can only have meaning in the context of the ongoing purposes of God, in the removing of hindrances to the advance of his kingdom. To claim it for our personal needs or healings pushes it right out of context. But for all of us who are engaged in the spiritual battle, wrestling against principalities and powers, and all the forces of darkness—whether in the pioneer mission field, the inner city, the materialistically-oriented suburbs or anywhere else —it is a powerful promise to claim.

Along with the prayer promises we need to take the great prayer ascription of Ephesians 3:20—a verse that has meant much to me in my ministry and in ventures of faith for the Lord: "Now to him who by the power at work within us is able to do far more abundantly than all that we ask or think, to him be glory in the church and in Christ Jesus to all generations, for ever and ever. Amen." It is the climax of Paul's prayer for the Ephesians—a prayer for spiritual growth and maturity, for supernatural strength and power. How Paul longs for the church to increase in its impact! His ascription shows that he sets no limits on what can happen.

The phrase "far more abundantly" is vividly pictorial. Its basic derivation is the word *perisseuo*—to overflow. Paul never thought in terms of a dribble of blessing. He always expected a fountain! But Greek words may be strengthened by adding prefixes to them. So Paul puts an *ek* in front of the word. That makes it a *great* overflowing—pouring over and flooding out. But even that is not enough for him. So he puts *huper* in front of all that! Now the word is a veritable Niagara Falls of blessing, with no limit to what God can do, except us: "by the power at work *within us*." How often does a church or a Christian work miss out on what God can do because they do not trust him as God, because they limit their prayers to what they think he can cope with, and so live in spiritual puddles instead of under the waterfall of grace!

Look at the ascription again—this overflowing blessing is "more than all that we ask or think." Some years ago an oil company was offering "Bizzy pens" (felt-tip pens) with any purchase of its gasoline. Our children were younger then, and their enthusiasm for this particular free offer dictated what brand of gas we bought! We were travelling with our two boys to Scotland. Just across the Forth Bridge we came to a gas station advertising Bizzy pens. Delight in the back of the car! We filled up. "The pens please," they asked.

"Ouch! They're all gone," replied the attendant.

The boys were indignant. "Can we put the gas back?"

Some days later we needed to fill up again. This time we were more careful. We asked first and the Scottish garage-owner carefully doled out one Bizzy pen for each four gallons purchased. On our way home through England the Bizzy pen garages seemed few and far between. The gas gauge was near zero. The situation was tense! "We'll have to stop at the next garage whatever gas they sell," I said. There was reluctant agreement in the back of the car. We were climbing a long hill. Suddenly, over the horizon there appeared the top of the favored gasoline company's sign. Excitement grew. Gradually the pole beneath it came into view. Sure enough, there was the sign: "Bizzy pens." The boys were on their feet cheering. As soon as we pulled in they approached the pump attendant. "How many Bizzy pens can we have?"

"As many as you like," he said.

That was good enough for our youngsters who staggered back to the car with arms full! That is what *huper-ek-perisseuo* means—super overflowing, more than you ask or think! How like our God. He is not one to dole out one blessing for every four good deeds, or one who runs out of blessings altogether, but a God who wants to see his church go forward praying, expecting, daring, believing, so that he can match it all with his overflowing blessing—and the glory will be his.

So, if we are to understand prayer, we must *start with God*. We must lay firmly the foundations: of faith in God as God—God in the center, of the character of God in his holiness and love, of the purposes of God being worked out year by year, of the ways of God in rich and sometimes surprising variety. Next, we must build onto those foundations the great prayer promises. Then we must stand up and affirm to him our trust in his power and our desire for his glory—as the God who by the power at work within us is able to do far more abundantly than all that we ask or think —a *huper-ek-perisseuo* God! To him be glory in the church and in Christ Jesus to all generations, for ever and ever. Amen!

2
GETTING CLOSE
TO GOD

CHAPTER 7

APPROACHING GOD WITH WORSHIP

THERE ARE MANY PATTERNS FOR US TO ADOPT in our approach to God. Possibly the best known is A-C-T-S: adoration, confession, thanksgiving, supplication. The patterns put our own requests last; they all begin with worship.

"Approach patterns" in prayer

It is said that Dr. R. A. Torrey found his experience transformed when he learned not only to pray and thank but to worship, to spend time not only asking but being "occupied with God." Many Christians do not start here—indeed they hardly know what worship means. Take the average church service. Some people enter the church only a minute before the beginning of the service, or even after it has started. They follow the various prayers, hymns, and scriptures; they give some attention to the sermon. After the benediction they go outside and join in the hubbub of conversation about Billy's new girl friend and Sheila's new car.

But where is God in it all? Is there any sense of coming to meet with the living Lord, with wonder, awe, and adoration? Is there any expectancy, any anticipation of God's blessing, conviction, or challenge? Does a stranger coming into the church sense that God is being worshiped? It is so easy for any of us to slide into a slipshod and irreverent performance called "worship." The same is too easily true of our personal prayer time. It can become just a fragment of our day, fitted in between the other urgent demands, its content a shopping list which we rattle off without any real consciousness of the presence of the Lord.

So, what is worship?
Worship is, of course, "worth-ship"—giving God the glory and honor which is due to him. At the same time it is an expression of our dependence upon him and our submission to him as Lord. Frequently in Scripture, worship is associated with falling down, or kneeling. This practice was not confined to Jews or Christians. You will recall that the decree of King Nebuchadnezzar, in Daniel 3:10, required everyone to "fall down and worship the gold image." It was completely natural for the wise men, when they came into the house where the child Jesus was, to "fall down and worship." When Satan tempted Jesus to submit to his "authority," he took Jesus up on a high mountain and showed him the kingdoms of the world in all their glory and proclaimed "All these I will give you, if you fall down and worship me." When Peter arrived at the house of Cornelius he was embarrassed because Cornelius knelt and worshiped *him*. Kneeling is a physical demonstration of submission to the authority and superiority of another. Because there is no greater authority in heaven and earth than the Lord's and no one superior to him, it is our duty

and privilege to respond to the exhortation of Psalm 95:6-7 "O come, let us worship and bow down, let us kneel before the LORD our Maker! For he is our God, and we are the people of his pasture and the sheep of his hand."

How do we worship?
Two important verses will guide us in our attitude to worship: "God is Spirit, and those who worship him must worship in spirit and truth" (John 4:24). "I appeal to you therefore, brethren, by the mercies of God, to present your bodies as a living sacrifice, holy and acceptable to God, which is your spiritual worship" (Rom. 12:1).

Three areas of our beings are capable of responding to God: our spirit, our mind, and our body. Real worship will consciously involve all three.

Worshiping in spirit When Jesus spoke to the woman at the well (John 4:7-26) he knew that her "worship" was a formal activity defined by what was done and how it was done. Jesus pressed her right to the heart of a truer worship. No form of service, however good, is worship—it is only the vehicle of worship. In Jesus Christ a new dimension of spiritual worship was to be opened up, in which men and women would be indwelt by the Holy Spirit, who would inspire, enlighten, and empower them from within. This is the privilege of every Christian. We must therefore take time to tune in to the Spirit of God within us as we approach the Lord. We cannot just charge into his presence and deliver our requests. We must come without hurry, asking the Holy Spirit to open up our hearts. As he does, he will witness with our spirit that we are the children of God, he will glorify Jesus, he will take the things of God and open them to us, he will interpret spiritual truth to us, he will draw forth our deepest adoration and worship—often without words. Or by taking the words of Scripture or hymns he will release our hearts to make their words our own expressions of worship. Whether on our own in daily devotion or in a church service or corporate worship the Holy Spirit takes all these elements and lifts us through them and above them in spiritual worship.

This spiritual dimension is eternal—it unites us with the whole of heaven. Hebrews 12:22-24 lifts the curtain for us. When we come to the Lord in worship, it says, we are coming to "Mount Zion and to the city of the living God, the heavenly Jerusalem, and to innumerable angels in festal gathering, and to the assembly of the firstborn who are enrolled in heaven, and to a judge who is God of all, and to the spirits of just men made perfect, and to Jesus the media- tor of the new covenant." Here we are, on our knees in our bedroom or sharing in the service on a Sunday, yet we are an integral part of the vast family of God in heaven. We are citizens of heaven, in exile for the moment, but united by the Holy Spirit to the eternal family to which we belong. So we often say in the Communion service: "With angels and archangels and with all the company of heaven, we proclaim your great and glorious name; evermore praising you and saying: 'Holy, holy, holy Lord, God of power and might, heaven and earth are full of your glory.' "

Worshiping with the mind Jesus added the words "and in truth" to what he said about worship in John 4:23. There was much error in the Samaritans' religion, as there was in the pharisaism of some of the Jews. Jesus was constantly exposing error and teaching truth. In much of his teaching ministry he used parables and stories to illustrate, but he never watered down the truth itself. "I am the way, the truth and the life," he said in John 14:6. Men had to face up to that truth and sometimes it was too strong for them. In John 6:66, after his teaching about the need to partake of his body and blood, "many of his disciples drew back and no longer went about with him." Jesus asked the twelve: "Will you also go away?" and Peter answered: "Lord, to whom shall we go? You have the words of eternal life." Al- though the truth divides, it also liberates: "If you continue

in my word, you are truly my disciples, and you will know
the truth and the truth will make you free" (John 8:31-32).
The church from Pentecost onwards has sought to teach,
spread, and protect the truth of God. Mindless worship is
contrary to the Spirit of the New Testament and those
engaged even in the "ecstatic" worship of 1 Corinthians 14
were told: "In thinking be mature" (verse 20).

Worship must therefore include the submission of our
minds to the wisdom of God—to his thoughts, which are
higher than our thoughts. Meditation on the Scriptures,
with an open mind and prayerful attitude, is essential
within our daily worship. But whether we follow a pre-
determined system of Bible reading, or create our own
pattern, the object will be deeper than a mere intellectual
understanding of the Word. Notes and commentaries may
help us but personal, prayerful meditation is vital. We must
ask ourselves, "What is the Lord saying to me in this passage, today? How am I to respond, to be a doer of the Word
and not a hearer only? What does the passage also show me
of my God, his character, and ways? Is there a particular
truth or verse which so inspires me that I may carry it into
my praying and on through the day?"

The truth of God must also be a check on our forms of
worship. We cannot worship God acceptably if our attitude
is "anything goes." He is to be worshiped "in truth" as well
as "in spirit," and however much we may want to share in
friendship or dialogue with people of other religions, for
instance, our commitment to the truth revealed for us by
the Son of God will make us wary of multi-faith "acts of
worship." Those of us who belong to churches with a liturgical pattern of worship will also be concerned that we use
liturgies in accord with the truth of God. We will find it
painful when expressions contrary to that truth are in-
serted. (Non-liturgical services often sit even more lightly
to the truth!) In our times of personal or corporate worship
we must mean what we say to God; our minds must gladly

affirm his revealed truth and submit to it; and there should always be a measure of transformation of our lives by the renewing of our minds.

Worshiping with the body The body part of worship is the submission of my life to my Lord, putting myself entirely at my commanding officer's disposal and ready to do his will. My daily acts of worship need to include this surrender, laying my life at the Lord's feet for this day—for its work, its relaxation, its decisions, its conversations, its joys and sorrows, its opportunities for witness and service and for all the "unknowns" ahead of me each day. This is a deliberate expression to God of my submission to his purposes and his ways.

Such submission is movingly demonstrated by David in 2 Samuel 12:20. After he had given himself to fasting and prayer for the recovery of his child by Uriah's wife, Bathsheba, the child died. Then "David arose from the earth, and washed and anointed himself, and changed his clothes; and he went into the house of the LORD and *worshiped*." Only then did he go to his own house to eat. The child's death was a judgment on David's appalling sin against Uriah, but even in that David submitted and worshiped. I ask myself whether that would be how I would react to judgment or to a deep sorrow or bereavement. Is my life a life of worship?

There will be other times of worship, however, when I will want to dedicate my life anew to God's service, submitting to his overall direction and purpose. In such moments the whole course of life may be changed as God opens up new avenues of service, or calls me out of my present job to go for him to another part of the world. In such moments also he may confirm his present calling to stay where I am to continue serving him here. Either way, it involves the submission of my body in worship. Whoever we are, we only have one life to live for God on this earth. Let it be the life he wants!

Preparing for corporate worship

In corporate worship we are able to focus the attitude of worship and find inspiration from sharing together. At least, that is the ideal—the reality may fall far short of that because of ourselves or because of the service itself.

Let's start with ourselves. If worship involves my spirit, mind, and body, I cannot expect to "tune in" to a service of worship without preparation. People who get up late, rush to church, and arrive just before or after the service begins are in no state to worship the living God. The service will probably seem "dead" or "cold" to them and afterwards they may be critical of the message or other parts of the service. But the fault is in themselves. Others have come out of church inspired and renewed, challenged and uplifted, because they took time to prepare themselves the night before or that morning before leaving home. They arrived in time to pray, to meditate, to be quiet before the Lord, to look through the hymns planned for the service so that later they could sing them with conviction and true worship. They came not "to attend church" or "to go to a service" but to meet with the Lord of heaven and earth and to worship him. Their anticipation and expectancy influenced the depth of their participation.

The other factor is the service itself. Sometimes our anticipation and expectancy is sadly blunted and disappointed by a service that seems to lack preparation or meaningful leadership. It may happen to us when we are away from home on a Sunday and visit a local church. Sometimes we feel joy and delight—the Lord is uplifted and no one doubts that he is there; sometimes we feel a deep sadness that there is so little life and reality. A considerable responsibility rests on those of us who lead services of worship. I was not trained to spend time planning services and it was a long while before it dawned on me that when care and prayer went into planning a service, the Lord of the Church would bring it powerfully to life. In the church to which I belong we plan our preaching series months in advance, praying and discussing, seeking to sense the right balance of the "preaching menu." Then one, two, or three hours a week are spent going through the hymn and psalm books, searching out the most appropriate and meaningful material to support a given preaching theme. Gradually the service takes on this thematic approach, even in the prayers, if that seems possible. The church family is urged to pray about the worship services—and does so together in the church prayer meeting. We all care deeply that every service will be a special service—the Lord meeting with us in his uniqueness.

When there is preparation of both the worshipers and the service, there will be living worship. What a glorious experience it can be to share oneness with the Lord and each other in the service of Holy Communion. Then there are the occasions when we have the benefit of great music. Singing "Crown Him with Many Crowns" the other night with our full church orchestra, I felt I needed only the slightest push to float into glory! But that can be true even with an out-of-tune piano or no music at all. The Lord may overwhelm us, as he did a young man who ran out of church because he felt the love of God so strongly he wanted to be alone. The Word of God may come powerfully to our minds and souls as it is preached or read, or as it is "lifted off the page" by music in an oratorio or anthem or solo. For others, worship may come alive when it is informal, with guitars to accompany the singing and many sharing. It is the Lord who makes it "real."

Corporate worship gives us special opportunities to be "occupied with God" and great Sundays overflow into great Mondays, maintaining our worship on through the week. In our daily quiet times with God our spirit, mind, and body can be inspired and refreshed by Sunday's worship. There will be joy, praise, adoration, all producing reverent submission.

"Therefore let us be grateful for receiving a kingdom that cannot be shaken, and thus let us offer to God acceptable worship, with reverence and awe, for our God is a consuming fire" (Heb. 12:28-29).

CHAPTER 8

APPROACHING GOD WITH PENITENCE

ALTHOUGH THERE MUST BE REVERENCE, awe, and wonder in our approach to God, there should certainly be no lack of *confidence*. Hebrews 10:19 uses the word plainly and encouragingly: "We have confidence to enter the sanctuary by the blood of Jesus." This confidence is based not on our worthiness but on Christ's and what he has done; he has opened for us "the new and living way," he is our great high priest, he offered, for all time, a single sacrifice for sins.

We are then, according to Hebrews 10:22, to "draw near with a true heart in full assurance of faith" but "with our hearts sprinkled clean from an evil conscience and our bodies washed with pure water." Whenever we come into the presence of God we come as sinners cleansed and forgiven through the blood of Christ. The worshiper must never forget the basis of his being welcomed by God, must never approach God in an attitude of self-confidence. Our confidence is solely in Christ, our Savior and Mediator.

The Holy Communion service vividly expresses, time and time again, for us and to God, that our salvation rests on the sacrifice made once for all upon the Cross. Whatever the season of the Church's year, we celebrate it in the broken body and poured-out blood of Christ. Here is our spiritual birthright for eternity. Here is our assurance and confidence.

The bath and the basin

However, there is a distinction between that once-for-all sacrifice for sins and the need to go on being forgiven. You remember how Jesus spelled this out to Peter in the Upper Room (John 13). Peter had refused to have his feet washed by Jesus, but Jesus insisted. He distinguished between bathing and foot-washing—or, in our terms, bathing and hand-washing. Peter's preliminary resistance to any washing by Jesus then gave way to a request to be bathed all over, but Jesus told him he had already been bathed and did not need to be bathed again. Modern-day Peters often want some fresh assurance of forgiveness or acceptance by God and will frequently seek to be "re-converted" or "re-blessed" at a service instead of accepting the fact of the "bath" once and for all. However, on the other side of the coin are those who emphasize the truth of the "bath" they know Christ has given them but give scant attention to the foot-washing. In the dusty dryness of the Near East, this practical action was necessary several times a day, just as handwashing is with us. The need for continued spiritual cleansing and forgiveness is also necessary every day—even several times a day. Are we careless about our spiritual hygiene?

We are well aware of the words in 1 John 1:8, 9, addressed to Christians: "If we say we have no sin, we deceive ourselves, and the truth is not in us. If we confess our sins,

APPROACHING GOD WITH PENITENCE

he is faithful and just, and will forgive our sins and cleanse us from all unrighteousness." Such forgiveness is possible because of the Cross and because we have an Advocate with the Father, Jesus Christ the righteous (1 John 2:1).

In the foot-washing incident and in his emphasis on forgiveness in the Lord's Prayer: "Forgive us our sins..." Jesus showed that he meant us to take this seriously. It is a truth which dawns slowly on us—the more we go on in the Christian life the more we see our sin and so the more we have to confess. Like Isaiah, as we see God's holiness and majesty, we also see our uncleanness in his light (Isa. 6:4). Our self-interest, self-opinion, self-centeredness and self-sufficiency become uncomfortably exposed. The shallowness of our love for God and our neighbor is known by contrast with the depth of his love for us. We increasingly see sin not just as a regrettable weakness of personal failure but as an offense against our Lord and God.

Sometimes it helps us to open up to one another, as in James 5:16: "Confess your sins to one another and pray for one another." This is not done lightly. Normally it would need to be in the security of a close friendship or small prayer group or in a confidential pastoral or counselling relationship. I have listened to many confessions—walking about a conference grounds, sitting in my study, sharing in a side pew of the church or out in the country—but always with the opportunity to minister the Word, to talk, and then to pray with and for the person concerned. The minister needs to be able to turn to others for similar fellowship, perhaps to a fellow-minister or to a good friend in the church fellowship.

Confession—preparing for worship

I am thankful to be in a church that includes confession as part of its normal liturgy. Some people do not like it—they dislike having to tell God they are sinners each time they come to worship. But perhaps that tells us more about their

spiritual pride than it does about the liturgy! In the days
before hymns the service opened with confessional state-
ments such as 1 John 1:8-9, or Psalm 51:17: "The sacrifice
acceptable to God is a broken spirit; a broken and contrite
heart, O God, thou wilt not despise," or Luke 15:18: "I will
arise and go to my father, and I will say to him, 'Father, I
have sinned against heaven and before you; I am no longer
worthy to be called your son.' " The liturgy then moved into
the exhortation about worship, emphasizing that we must
first admit and confess our sins. The Confession, in which
everyone joins, accurately puts first the sins of omission:
"We have failed to do what we ought to have done" before
the sins of commission: "We have done what we ought not
to have done." The emphasis is on the seriousness of sin,
the need for mercy and restoration.

When I go to church services where confession is either
ignored or merely alluded to in passing in the minister's
prayer, I sense a deep lack in the whole approach to God.
This is not just my feeling. There *is* a deep lack. If confession and forgiveness are not taken seriously in corporate
worship then they are unlikely to be taken seriously in personal prayer. As we saw earlier, what happens on Sundays
should inspire and guide the pattern of our approach to
God during the week. There should, however, be time for
reflection and self-examination before a service begins if
we are to join sincerely in the general act of confession—a
further stimulus to preparation beforehand. And in services which do not include a penitential opening we will
need to incorporate our own act of penitence in the quiet
of our hearts before the service begins.

A spiritual check-up
In our personal devotional prayer we should give more
time and attention to self-examination—which is not mor-
bid introspection but evidence of a real desire to walk more
worthily of our Lord, to repent of sin, and to know the joy

of his forgiveness. There are various books of devotion that can help us. Some people value Lancelot Andrewes' *Preces Privatae*. He certainly opens up a wide range of thinking about sin and forgiveness, but is rather lacking in joy. I find John Baillie's *A Diary for Private Prayer* immensely helpful because it seems to relate more to everyday living. All of us should have and use books like these but we may also find it helpful to prepare our own "spiritual check-up" book. For instance we might ask ourselves questions like these:

1 Can I listen to other Christian workers being praised and not be jealous?

2 Can I hear of the "success" of some other church or Christian work and not try to explain it away?

3 Can I be constructively criticized and not resent the criticizer?

4 Can I accept that my talents and gifts may be less noticed than gifts in some other Christians, even if they are just as useful for God?

5 What do I honestly regard as "making it" in life—is it in terms of Christian maturity or do I judge it by my possessions and success?

6 What is the overriding ambition of my life—to be "someone" or to serve Christ faithfully?

7 How much have I brought God into my thinking, planning, and doing today?

8 Is my love of God's Word growing cold?

9 How generously do I give? Have I analyzed my giving recently, testing it by the standard of a tenth or more?

10 Do I want to give the least I can or the most?

11 Am I an intercessor? Is it time to organize my praying, using a notebook, so that I can support many people and different aspects of the Lord's work in prayer?

12 Am I really concerned about the poverty of so much of the world and the social needs of my own city or town?

13 How can I describe my life-style? Is it Christ-focussed or hardly distinguishable from a non-Christian's? Is it a simple or materialistic and selfish one?

14 How good a listener am I to preaching and to the counsel or opinion of others?

15 Do I care about people—in my home, in my place of work, in my neighborhood?

16 Is my evangelism sensitive, treating the other person with respect and care, or do I bludgeon people with the gospel?

17 Am I prepared to let other people do the mundane jobs of moving chairs, preparing meals, and serving others while I converse?

18 How grateful am I for food—for its supply and its preparation?

19 Do I have a double standard—comfort for my home and austerity for my church?

20 Has any action or attitude of mine disgraced Christ this week? Has my temper flared? Have I acted selfishly or thoughtlessly?

21 Are there those who don't want to be part of the church because I am?

22 Am I prepared to speak up for Christ anywhere or am I sometimes ashamed or reluctant to be known as a Christian?

23 Did I really worship God last Sunday—or did I just go through the form of service?

24 Have people looked for Christ in me and been disappointed?

25 How much does the love of God flow through me to others?

26 Am I loyal to the body of Christ or do I needlessly criticize Christian things to unbelievers?

27 Am I scrupulously honest in my tax returns and my expense claims? Do I keep the speed limit?

28 Can people rely completely on my word?

29 Is my language clean? Are my relationships pure?
30 Am I quick to see the wrongs of others but slow to see my own?
31 Do I make allowances for my own failings but not for those of others?
32 Am I a peace-maker? Am I quick to say "I'm sorry"?
33 Am I tuned in to God's purpose for my life? If so, how well has that purpose been implemented this month?
34 Lord, how do *you* see my life? "Create in me a clean heart, O God, and put a new and right spirit within me" (Ps. 51:10).

We would do well to learn the "habit of penitence" as thoroughly as the habit of washing our hands. In the office when we "blow our top" over something we need to apologize to the people we have hurt. But what about God? Should we not pause, open our hearts to the Lord, and ask for his forgiveness there and then? We are reading a book or watching a film when something in it really "strikes home," showing us a fault in ourselves that we had overlooked or ignored. It should be a moment for reflection, and then for confession and forgiveness. God speaks to us in so many ways and the Holy Spirit may at any time convict us of selfishness or lack of love or anything that is not in keeping with Christian living. We must act on it, confess it, be cleansed.

Precursors to praise
True penitence is always met by our Lord with mercy and grace. It is a wonderful fact that our Lord has shared human life and well knows the problems of temptation. As Hebrews 4:15 says: Christ is "not a high priest who is unable to sympathize with our weaknesses." Confession and forgiveness will naturally be followed by praise and thanksgiving—with all the joy of a freshly cleansed conscience, to worship and serve him. There is a rhythm to the Chris-

tian life. Where sin is not taken seriously the Christian misses the liberating joy and blessing of sins confessed and forgiven. A Christian's existence without this pattern becomes monochromatic. He misses the depth of heartfelt praise expressed in so many hymns, for it is the one who is forgiven much who loves much, the one who sees the depth of God's mercy who is constantly inspired to praise:

> *Praise, my soul, the king of heaven;*
> *To his feet thy tribute bring.*
> *Ransomed, healed, restored, forgiven,*
> *Who like thee his praise should sing?*
> *Praise him, praise him.*
> *Praise the everlasting King!*

CHAPTER 9

APPROACHING GOD WITH PRAISE AND THANKSGIVING

PRAISE IS TO BE A CONSTANT DIMENSION in our Christian lives. "Through him (Jesus) then let us continually offer up a sacrifice of praise to God, that is, the fruit of lips that acknowledge his name." (Heb. 13:15). This text immediately reminds us that true praise is *to* God *through* Jesus, and is a *fruit* of our submission to him as Lord and Savior. So praise is *not* hymns, anthems, solos, psalms, songs, oratorios, or choruses. They are only the vehicles of praise. To join in hymns without a heart redeemed by the blood of Christ and renewed by the Holy Spirit is merely to sing words —it is not praise to the living God. The true desire and ability to "sing a new song to the Lord" depends not on a musical ability qualification but on a heart qualification (though it is a bonus if there is musical excellence as well!). The bursts of praise in Scripture are always heart-bursts.

What does it mean *"continually"* to "offer up a sacrifice of praise"? Such a sacrifice will spring naturally from an atmosphere of praise. My wife, Myrtle, comes from a family with many aunts and uncles. Her oldest uncle breathed a unique spirit of loving encouragement. Whenever you visited him he took a close interest in how things were going for you and that interest continued even when you could not visit. At the end of his life he entered a nursing home. When we went to visit him, he was full of admiration for the way the home was run, the kindness of all the nursing staff, the skill and care of the doctors, the help he received from everyone. "They are all wonderful," he said. Then we met some of the staff. "What a wonderful man he is," they said, "so cheerful and kind—we love to have him here." That summed it all up. His spirit of kindness and encouragement overflowed—it was continual. When there was opportunity to express gratitude he did so naturally, not as conventional courtesy.

So it is in the Christian life. We need to pray for an increasing spirit of praise and thanksgiving in our character and personality. Then, when there are specific opportunities to join in times of corporate praise or to express personal thanksgiving, they will be a natural expression of what is already in our hearts and not forced exercises. You see this in Jesus' life. As he takes the food to distribute to the five thousand he gives thanks—naturally. After the mission of the seventy and the disciples return full of what has happened, "in that same hour he rejoiced in the Holy Spirit and said 'I thank you, Father, Lord of heaven and earth, that you have hidden these things from the wise and understanding and revealed them to babes'" (Luke 10:21).

We see this in the early days of the Church. In Luke 24:52-53 we are told that after Jesus' ascension the disciples returned to Jerusalem with great joy and were continually in the temple praising God. And Acts 2:46 informs us that: "Day by day, attending the temple together and breaking bread in their homes, they partook of food with glad and generous hearts, praising God and having favor with all the people." A spirit of praise indeed! But then read what follows: "And the Lord added to their number day by day those who were being saved." It looks as if the spirit of praise was a powerful part of the process of evangelism. One popular view of Christianity is that it deprives us of the joy of living and that Christians face a life of legalism and misery. What a lie! When non-Christians see Christians around them who clearly have a spirit of praise it has an undeniable impact. We often find that when non-Christians come into our church, where a large number of people are genuinely worshiping and praising God from the heart, they are so moved by it that they begin to seek Christ. Not that we need to keep shouting "Hallelujah!" all the time or grinning artificially. Life includes much that is serious and sad, but the spirit of praise goes deep and it will be sensed, quietly there, even in the times of weeping and sorrow.

Praise for prayers answered

Naturally, praise will spring to our lips when we hear of something special God has done, or a blessing in a person's life, or an answer to prayer. When we were facing the re-building of All Souls church we found ourselves in a collision between the need for a building to serve the gospel and the interests of those who feel strongly about preserving historic buildings. My colleague, John Stott, had earlier expressed this ambivalence to a small meeting in Perth, western Australia, and had said it looked as if a bomb on the church would be the simplest solution! A reporter circulated the story, which received conspicuous coverage in the British press. Some years later, before the rebuilding actually commenced, the doorbell of the rectory rang. Two police officers were standing at the door. I invited them into the entrance hall. Solemnly they announced, "We have to inform you sir, that we have received a telephone call saying that a bomb has been planted in your church." Before I could think what I was saying, I responded: "Praise the Lord!" The police officers were somewhat taken aback! Even though the telephone call proved to be a hoax, it was a memorable moment!

Praise in the face of problems

A tougher test of the spirit of praise comes when we are facing the difficulties of life. The example of Paul and Silas beaten with rods, shut in the inner prison, their feet in the stocks, praying and singing hymns to God at midnight is an outstanding story of praise under difficult conditions. It is an example that thousands of other prisoners for the Lord have been enabled to follow down through Christian history and in the present day. Paul later wrote (1 Thess. 5:16-18): "Rejoice always, pray constantly, give thanks in all circumstances; for this is the will of God in Christ Jesus for you."

It is important to get this clear: "*in* all circumstances," not "*for* all circumstances." The idea of praising God for disasters, tragedies, and illnesses has gained currency amongst some Christians in recent years. It is put across as the way of high Christian living, of triumphant faith. But is this really what the Bible teaches?

One night the telephone rang. I listened as a father phoning long distance explained that his son was in great trouble—his marriage broken up, jobless, homeless, and an alcoholic. But I couldn't believe my ears. He was saying: "Of course, we are praising God that his marriage has broken up, he has no job, has nowhere to live, and is an alcoholic." My blood ran cold. Praising God for those things? That seemed more like a secular philosophy of positive thinking than a cause for Christian praise.

However, if we praise God *in* those circumstances rather than *for* them, then we are on a strong biblical footing. Look at the triumph of 1 Thessalonians 5:16-18. There is certainly biblical warrant for praise in all circumstances: praise that nothing can separate us from the love of God, that there is a way back to God for that homeless, jobless man in his marriage break-up and alcoholism. Yes! It is Christian to praise God in the midst of bereavement—praising him for his presence and comfort, praising him for his assurance of eternal life. It is Christian to praise God in illness—praising him that he has power to heal or bring other blessings out of this experience. It is Christian to praise God in disasters—praising him that he is with us in this experience and can bring his purposes to fruition through it all. But that is different from praising him *for* all circumstances.

But what about Ephesians 5:20, some will say? "Always and for everything giving thanks in the name of our Lord Jesus Christ to God the Father." This is certainly the spirit of praise—the verse is preceded by an exhortation to praise in music. But can this phrase "for everything" actually mean that I should thank God for someone who is living immorally, or for my friend being killed in a highway accident, or for a person going blind, or someone being cruel to his wife. If so, I am being asked to give praise for evil and nowhere in the Scriptures is such a thing countenanced. The very opposite is true and verses 3-13 of this chapter of Ephesians spell it out: "Immorality and all impurity must not be named among you ... because of these things the wrath of God comes upon the sons of disobedience ... walk as children of the light [for the fruit of the light is found in all that is good and right and true] ... take no part in the unfruitful works of darkness, but instead *expose* them." Evil is to be avoided or fought, or exposed. Death is "an enemy" (1 Cor. 15:26). Remember, when the devil is cast finally into the lake of fire we shall not say: "Praise the Lord for the devil," but "Praise the Lord—evil has been conquered for ever."

The idea behind praising for cruelty and wrong, some

say, is that it shows we trust that God is in control. But such trust is basic to Christian conviction in any case. We *do* believe he is Lord and that "in everything God works for good with those who love him, who are called according to his purpose" (Rom. 8:28). We testify to the way in which he has brought good out of evil, blessing out of disaster, and healing out of sickness. We do not have to give praise for evil to demonstrate this conviction. Jesus never did, nor did any of the apostles.

Christ, the heart of our praise
The key to triumph is in being able to separate the problem or circumstance from our spirit of praise. Let me explain. When the seventy returned from their mission in Luke 10:17-20 full of praise for what had happened, Jesus said to them: "Do not rejoice in this, that the spirits are subject to you, but rejoice that your names are written in heaven." The fount of praise is constant—it springs from our salvation and our security in the Lord. If it is in circumstances then it will go fly "high" or drop "low" according to what is happening to us. Like a car without the clutch depressed, the engine and gears are so linked that the engine will stall at low speeds. The clutch brings release to the engine from the gears and allows it to run even when the car is waiting at a traffic light. When we learn to "use the clutch" in our Christian lives, in *all* circumstances, we will be "continually" offering the sacrifice of praise. To put it simply, the Christian cannot say "Everything's awful. I can't praise," nor "Everything's awful, praise the Lord!" nor "Everything's awful, praise the Lord for the awfulness," but "Everything's awful, but I give praise because I know the Lord is with me in this experience and will carry me through. Praise the Lord."

When my wife and I were in the United States at a conference last year, I was speaking on this theme. Afterwards a couple came up to me saying, "We can't wait to telephone our daughter. She has been diagnosed a diabetic and we have constantly told her that she will not get the victory until she praises God for her diabetes. But every time she replies, "I can't." Now we are going to tell her she needn't do so, but can have victory through praising God *in* her diabetic state." I hope that girl has found the power to praise God *in* all circumstances.

Let us pray for the Holy Spirit to deepen the fount of praise and thanksgiving in our lives, that it may be a continual witness to the Lord's grace. Then when opportunity arises to praise him specially, lifting our hearts to him several times during the day, or as we come together with other Christians, or as we kneel alone to meet with him, let us praise him out of the depths of our thankful hearts. Sometimes that will be in the quietness of awe and adoration. It may be as in Ezra 3 at the foundation of the temple rebuilding, when the older people wept with joy while the younger ones shouted. It may be with great music, with organ and orchestras. It may be informally with guitars, choruses, and spiritual songs. It may be in spontaneous phrases of praise. It may be in giving for the Lord's work —giving of our money and time. It may be in renewed lives of commitment. We may use hymns, psalms, poems, songs, recorded music, devotional books of praise. We may compile our own anthologies of praise. But let us, through Christ, continually offer up a sacrifice of praise to God, that is, the fruit of lips that acknowledge his name. Keep praising!

If our praise and thanksgiving is not to get into a rut, we need to refresh it often and extend its range of content. It is appropriate to ask next: for what do we praise? I found my praising widened in scope and enriched in depth when I worked through the Scriptures and found six main themes of praise:

Praise for God himself
We are to praise God as God—revelling in the wonder of

who he is and all that he means to us. Such praise abounds in the heart of the psalmist: "I call upon the Lord, who is worthy to be praised" (Ps. 18:3);

"Who is God, but the Lord? And who is a rock, except our God?" (Ps. 18:31);

"O Lord, our Lord, how majestic is your name in all the earth!" (Ps. 8:1);

"The Lord reigns; he is robed in majesty; the Lord is robed, he is girded with strength . . . Your throne is established from of old; you are from everlasting." (Ps. 93);

"O come, let us sing to the Lord . . . for the Lord is a great God . . . he is our God" (Ps. 95);

"O sing to the Lord a new song; sing to the Lord, all the earth!" (Ps. 96);

"Great is the Lord and greatly to be praised . . . ascribe to the Lord the glory due to his name" (Ps. 96).

Here is a constant bubbling-over of adoration. It is the joy of the child in his wonderful Father. It is the glory of the fact that he who has made us his children forever is God —loving, powerful, and with no human limitations or fallibility, who will fulfill his word and one day gather his vast redeemed family to be with him in the new heavens and the new earth. As we live in a world where we wonder what is going to happen next, where international events move with breathless rapidity, where political powers exercise their perogatives, often with terrible effects, we can stand back, look up, and see things in perspective again. Whatever man does, nothing can separate us from God. He is King; he is Lord; and he is in control. So often I find myself simply revelling in God. And when I have the opportunity to do so in a large crowd of believing people, singing his praise with all my heart, that is marvelous! "King of kings and Lord of lords—Alleluia!" But often I will enjoy him when I am alone, walking down the street, or meditating on his Word, or waking up to a new day. He is God, and worthy to be praised. And as I see, in some new way, his character—his steadfast love, his faithfulness, his patience, his mercy, his kindness, his righteousness, his power—I am again stimulated to praise him. The more we know God, the more we will want to praise him.

Praise for creation
The psalmist lived nearer to the evidences of God's creation than those of us who live in cities. He had an eye for the touch of the Lord:

Psalm 19: "The heavens are telling the glory of God; and the firmament proclaims his handiwork."

Psalm 24: "The earth is the Lord's and the fullness thereof."

In Psalm 29 he observes the storm in the forest: "The voice of the Lord is upon the waters; the voice of the Lord breaks the cedars; the voice of the Lord makes the oaks to whirl, and strips the forest bare; and in his temple all cry 'Glory!' "

Or the great Psalm 104, so full of loving appreciation for the majesty of God's creation: "O Lord, how manifold are your works! In wisdom you have made them all; the earth is full of your creatures." The song of the seraphim in Isaiah 6 exults in the beauty of creation: "Holy, holy, holy is the Lord of hosts; the whole earth is full of his glory." And we look forward to sharing in the heavenly praise (Rev. 4:11): "Worthy are you, our Lord and God, to receive glory and honor and power, for you created all things, and by your will they existed and were created."

Even if you have grown up with an appreciation of beauty in creation, when you come to a living faith in Christ you see it all in new depth and with fresh meaning. As the hymn puts it, earth beneath becomes "sweeter green" and sky above "softer blue." This happens because instead of just admiring the beauty you begin to praise the *Creator* of the beauty. Whether standing on a mountain top, gazing across the valleys to the gigantic peaks around you, or seeing the wonder of growth in a seedling bravely flourishing in a windowbox, your heart praises the Creator.

It is a surprise to find that not everyone appreciates the beauty of the earth—not even all Christians. Coming out of the city of Manchester years ago, we headed for the Peak district with a party of city youths. We climbed to the top of Mam Tor and gazed across the marvelous panorama of hills and valleys. In the far distance we could glimpse a cement factory and a chimney belching smoke. "Ah, reality!" remarked one of the fellows with satisfaction. We accompanied another group for a holiday in some of the lovelier parts of southern England. Time and again we would pause while driving along and say: "Look at that!" The view thrilled my wife and myself, but not our passengers. "Yeah?" they replied and went on with their conversation. Part of our Christian responsibility is to help people to open up to the wonders of creation—to the striking, the lovely, the beautiful phenomena around us. It is good for Christians to develop hobbies and interests such as birdwatching, mountain-climbing, walking, and vacationing in places of scenic beauty. It is good that they develop an interest in music, in design, and all kinds of artistic expression. There is so much which is sordid around us, resulting from the effects of sin, that we need to make an effort to enjoy the lovely things of the world. For city dwellers this will mean more frequent trips out of the city so as to keep a balance in life.

Increasingly, the joy of creation will inspire us to praise —the first buds of spring on the trees, the first new flowers after the winter, the kaleidoscope of colors in the trees of autumn, the magnificence of a sunset, the delicacy of frost on the window, the contours of mountains, lakes, and forests, the rich variety of animal life, the miracles of birth and growth, the resources of the earth, the ability to create and invent, life itself in all its fullness. Think of the Creator and enter the wide arena of praise!

We will want to make this a deliberate part of our regular pattern of praise and thanksgiving as well as the spontaneous praise of the moment of seeing. Think back over each day to what you have seen of God's manifold creation —in the large and the small—and bring him your thanksgiving.

In the beautiful town of Olney, Buckinghamshire, John Newton and William Cowper wrote hymns and poems that continue to move us centuries later. The town is set beside the River Ouse, with old cottages and a tall-spired church surrounded by meadows, trees, and flowers. In this setting, William Cowper wrote, in "The Task":

> *Happy who walks with him! Whom what he finds*
> *Of flavour or of scent in fruit or flow'r*
> *Or what he views of beautiful or grand*
> *In nature, from the broad, majestic oak*
> *To the green blade that twinkles in the sun,*
> *Prompts with remembrance of a present God!*

Praise for the Word

In Psalm 19, praise for God's general revelation of himself through creation is matched by praise for God's special revelation revealing of his laws and ways. Verses 7 and 8 exclaim "The law of the Lord is perfect, reviving the soul ... the precepts of the Lord are right, rejoicing the heart." Psalm 119 is an anthem of praise for all that God's Word can mean to our lives. The Word directs our praise: "I will praise you with an upright heart, when I learn your righteous ordinances" (v. 7). It enriches us: "In the way of your testimonies I delight as much as in all riches" (v. 14). It is a constant source of praise: "At midnight I rise to praise you, because of your righteous ordinances: (v. 62) "Seven times a day" (v. 164).

Of course, the psalmist is not praising just for the Word itself but for the way it brings him hope, assurance, comfort, guidance, strength, and understanding. By obeying the Word he proves God's faithfulness, steadfast love, and righteousness. The Word is to him better than riches and sweeter than honey. He loves the law—the Word—and meditates upon it.

We are hardly likely to want to praise God for his Word unless we have approached it in love and obedience. An arm's-length relationship with the Scriptures, a polite respect for them, an intellectual understanding, without submission to their truth, a selective use of them as it suits us, or a manipulation of them to support our own theories or presuppositions—none of these will produce praise.

It is when the Word becomes the living Word to us that we begin to praise God. I was in my twenties before I turned to the Lord in sincerity and commitment. My Christianity before that had not been insincere, not without some study of the Bible, but it had to be "for real." This became true as the promised re-birth of the Holy Spirit opened me up to God, at the same time opening me to his Word. I suddenly began to "hunger for the Word," sitting up late into the night to read it.

Imagine this world without the Word of God brought to us "in many and various ways and in these last days spoken to us by his Son," this Word which proves itself as God's Word when we trust it and seek to obey it, this Word which has given authority to the Christian message, been the means of millions of people coming into salvation, the guide and teacher of the truth and ways of our God, and a comfort to so many. What other book could we turn to every day of our lives and find fresh inspiration as the Holy Spirit opens it up to us?

If we love the Word of God, then let us praise him for it —praise him when he has shown us something new in our meditation on it, or when he has convicted us of sin or challenged us to action, or when he has revealed more of himself and his character to us, or when he has brought it to life for someone else we have been counselling, or when he has reminded us of his truth in a moment of need. Let us praise and thank the Lord for the Bible and show our praise by being doers of the Word and not hearers only.

Praise for salvation
A never-ending source of praise is our salvation. In the Old Testament, redemption from slavery brought forth frequent praise. Again and again God delivered his people because of his steadfast love. For us, as New Testament believers, redemption is in Christ, who delivers us from the slavery of sin, reconciling God with man, opening the gate of eternal life. We worship Christ by using that special title "Savior," with which his birth was announced to the world. It is heart-rending that some Christians react negatively to the word "save." Perhaps they do so because of some unfortunate misuse of the word or because they associate it with a particular form of evangelism. But if they do so they avoid one of the greatest words of the Christian faith. Even today, in our daily newspapers, the word "save" still means a rescue, a snatching from destruction. We use it of people saved from a sinking ship or a car accident or a house on fire. Perhaps the word only means much to us when we realize from what we have been saved, when we see clearly the division between perishing and living eternal life (John 3:16), between destruction and life (Matt. 7:13-14) or between condemnation and salvation (John 3:17).

When John Newton composed his hymn "Amazing Grace" at Olney he wrote it as a man who had known the depths of sin before coming to Christ. From a full heart of praise sprung the words:

> *Amazing grace! (how sweet the sound!)*
> *That saved a wretch like me!*
> *I once was lost, but now am found,*
> *Was blind, but now I see.*

There was a time when I could not have echoed those words. One night the minister of the church where I was a youth said in the middle of his sermon: "Stand up, all who know they are saved!" After the service there was a furor! "How dare those people stand up! How presumptuous of them—none of us will know we are saved until the judgment day." It was only slowly that I began to see that the presumption was not on the part of those who stood but of those who criticized. Clearly the critics were relying on themselves for salvation, while those who stood acknowledged that they could never be good enough for God and so, as sinners, had put their trust in Christ's sacrifice for their sins on the Cross. They "presumed" on Christ— exactly as God intended. When I saw this, I could begin to share John Newton's praise.

Salvation will be one of the two greatest themes of praise in heaven. As we praise God as our Creator, we will also sing to Jesus, the Lamb of God: "Worthy are you . . . for you were slain and by your blood you ransomed men for God, from every tribe and tongue and people and nation, and made them a kingdom and priests to our God" (Rev. 5:9-10).

This praise also bursts out in the New Testament. 1 Peter 1:3-9 is a hymn of praise for redemption: "Blessed be the God and Father of our Lord Jesus Christ!" Peter praises God for mercy, for being born anew to a living hope, for an inheritance in heaven, for the salvation of our souls.

This praise is echoed in our services and liturgy. The great celebration of the Holy Communion is described as a "sacrifice of praise and thanksgiving." We come to a Christian funeral service with a high note of triumphant praise even amid the sadness of bereavement, because death has lost its sting in Christ's death and resurrection and we rejoice in the living hope of eternal life. Thousands of hymns and poems have been written glorying in our salvation. It is a constant theme of praise. Let it be so in our lives. Let us never tire individually and corporately of praising God for his salvation.

Praise for God's actions in our behalf

Specific praise and specific thanks follow God's specific interventions or answers to prayer or blessings in the life of the biblical writers and Christians through the centuries.

"I waited patiently for the Lord; he inclined to me and heard my cry. He drew me up from the desolate pit . . . set my feet upon a rock. . . . He put a new song in my mouth, a song of praise to our God" (Ps. 40:1-3).

In 2 Corinthians 1:8-11 Paul writes of the afflictions he has had to face but praises God for the comfort received and the deliverance given. He goes on to urge the Corinthians to join in helping by prayer so that when God answers many will be able to share in the thanksgiving.

We all tend to be like the boy out visiting the home of friends with his mother. They sit down to tea. In the center of the table is a huge cream and chocolate cake. The boy is quietly told by his mother that he cannot start with the cake. He eats the sandwiches dutifully. At last, time for cake. The hostess cuts a piece and passes it to him. "What do you say?" prompts his mother. "Got it!" comes the reply. Too often we are like this with God. We pray about all sorts of things. We ask. We receive. But how often do we give specific thanks?

As we end the day, we should deliberately think back through its events, particularly those for which we have prayed in the morning, and give thanks. Some people keep a special prayer diary in which they record various requests, including prayer requests from others. On the opposite page they record the answers. Such a record must trigger our thanksgiving.

In our church gatherings for prayer we must start with praise and thanksgiving. The leader should keep notes from previous meetings so that he can share the specific

answers given, and others around the room should share
their own specific thanksgivings. It is enormously encouraging to share in thanksgiving like this, for the way God
has healed, for specific answers to prayer for an evangelistic service, for help in finding a job or somewhere to live,
for particular experiences of God's upholding. Some people also have an extra-special time of thanksgiving on their
birthday or the last day of the year or at some other significant anniversary. They look back and thank the Lord.

As the psalmist says (Ps. 107:1): "Give thanks to the Lord,
for he is good, for his steadfast love endures for ever!"

Praise for people
One of the surprises to me in researching the themes of
praise was that Paul frequently thanked God for his friends.
In his letters to the Romans, 1 Corinthians, Ephesians,
Philippians, Colossians, in both Thessalonian letters, in
both letters to Timothy, and Philemon, he gives thanks for
some characteristic of those to whom he is writing, even
when he is about to correct or criticize them. I find this chal-
lenging. I am much more ready to jump into criticism of
someone without looking for items to praise about them!
Paul is thankful for their faith, their service, their friendship, their partnership in the gospel, their love, their salvation. The spirit of praise keeps coming to the surface in
Paul's writing.

In praise for my friends I found a new dimension of
prayer. Of course I had done so before, but now I began to
thank God with more thought and a far wider coverage of
people.

We need to let our minds range across our friends and
colleagues, and our fellow churchmembers whom we meet
but who are not close friends. We can gather into our
thanksgiving leaders and helpers, observing and giving
thanks for acts of kindness, thoughtfulness, generosity,
encouragement, faithfulness. We need to learn to praise for

good qualities and deeds even in people whom we find it difficult to get along with. Thank the Lord for those who visit house-to-house this week, those who make the coffee after morning service, those who care for the elderly and the children, those who clean the church and stack the chairs, those who work long hours preparing for preaching, those young people standing up for God and his truth against mocking and opposition at college—the list is endless. Look around and widen your thanksgiving and praise for people!

One of the richest expressions of thanksgiving is in "the General Thanksgiving." It would be good to use it frequently as a summary of our thanking and praising:

Almighty God, Father of all mercies,

We your unworthy servants give you our humble and heartfelt thanks for all your goodness and loving kindness to us and to all men.

We praise you for our creation, preservation, and all the blessings of this life, but above all for your amazing love in the redemption of the world by our Lord Jesus Christ, for the means of grace and for the hope of glory.

We pray that you will give us such an awareness of your goodness that our hearts may be truly thankful, and that we may declare your praise not only with our lips but in our lives, by giving ourselves in your service and by walking before you in holiness and righteousness all our days.

All honour and glory be to you, Father, Son and Holy Spirit, now and throughout eternity. Amen.

CHAPTER 10

APPROACHING GOD AS CHILD TO FATHER

THE INVITATION TO CALL GOD "FATHER" was made by Jesus himself. We take it almost for granted, yet what a privilege it is! The title in all its richness deflects us from treating God with irreverent "chumminess." The Lord's Prayer follows the title "Father" with "hallowed be thy name" and directs us away from such a lack of reverence. Yet to be entitled, through Jesus, to call the living God "Father"—coming to him as his child, speaking to him with the openness of a child to a Father—is a wonderful intimacy. Revel in this relationship and all it means!

The concept was spelled out for us by Jesus in Luke 11. There he taught his followers "The Lord's Prayer" and went on to show us three things about the Father's attitude to us as his children.

A loving relationship

As sons to a Father (v. 11), as children to a Father (v. 13), so are we to our God. The term "children of God" is not used here in the sense of referring to all humanity. Indeed, the New Testament frequently emphasizes that in Christ the Father-son terminology is to be applied to the special relationship of God to the believer.

In John's prologue (John 1:12): "But to all who received him, who believed in his name, he gave power to become children of God," the meaning is crystal clear, as is Romans 8:15-17, speaking of life in the Spirit after being justified by faith: "You have received the Spirit of sonship. When we cry 'Abba! Father!' it is the Spirit himself bearing witness with our spirit that we are children of God." In the deep glorying of 1 John 3:1 the relationship is described: "See what love the Father has given us, that we should be called children of God; and so we are." When we believed in Christ we were made part of the Father's family, adopted children, his for ever. I hope you are sure of this in your own life and that the joy of it frequently overwhelms you —perhaps in the depth of real Christian fellowship, benefiting from brothers and sisters in Christ whose love is genuine and practical, perhaps in the delight of worship as part of his family or perhaps in moments when he seems to touch you with some special token of his love.

In a human family we usually share a lot of time together —eating, vacationing, discussing, and planning as a family. My daughter and sons have always been able to slip into my study to tell me if their bicycle chain has fallen off or to ask a question, or to sit in the kitchen chatting with their mother. Such togetherness is not always convenient, but it is part of family life.

Our God wants us to have a similar relationship with him. He is our "heavenly Father" and that word "heavenly" does not mean "remote," but that he is not restricted like an earthly father, that he is always ready to hear and his answers are always perfect.

It was at theological college that I first began to "see" this relationship. Some of my fellow students were clearly on much more open terms with God than I had known. Although worship and prayer meant a lot to me, I tended to keep them in their special slots. These fellows would pray about a letter or an essay or a problem and would *expect* the Lord to answer. And he seemed to do so! They talked to God about all sorts of things and at any time of the day. They simply "slipped into his study" as sons to a Father.

I still have much to learn about developing this relationship. I'm more likely to pray when I am meeting a crisis or when there is some special joy or encouragement, than I am in the more normal course of events. I need to make a conscious resolve to share everything with my Father—facing an interview, making a journey, looking for a place to park, coping with limited finances, getting things done when there seems too much to do in a short time, remembering a friend who is having an operation or taking an exam, turning world news into prayer.

Such a relationship also opens me up to my Father's correction and discipline—"The Lord disciplines him whom he loves" (Heb. 12:6). I can hardly bring things to him in prayer if I am consciously doing things which are against his truth and standards or in defiance of his guidance.

It is the privilege of all this which overwhelms me constantly. This infinitesimal piece of humanity is invited and encouraged to come at any time to the God who made the whole universe, the "I am" of eternity, and call him "Father." It's simply marvelous.

A loving readiness
Jesus must have been a vivid storyteller. He used such everyday illustrations that his hearers identified with them readily and so remembered what he said. The story he tells us in Luke 11:5 has always been one that has lived for me

—the knocking at the door of a friend at midnight to ask for bread. Poor fellow—fast asleep and snug, suddenly waking up and trying to think straight. How well we all know the feeling! Parents know it when the baby cries in the night and one has to get out of bed while the other turns over and goes back to sleep! It is a hazard of the ministry to get wakened up occasionally in the night (but not as often as doctors are). One night when we were in Manchester the doorbell rang and rang. It was about 3 A.M. I eventually woke up and realized the noise was the doorbell. I proceeded to stagger out of bed, find slippers and robe, put on lights, get the front door keys and make my way down the staircase of the big old rectory to the front door, where a man was standing. I noticed that the floodlights were still on, lighting up the church beside the rectory (we had obviously forgotten to turn them off when going to bed). As I opened the door, the man said: "Is your spire really as tall as it looks?"

So I have sympathy with the man in Jesus' story! He was an earthly father and it needed a considerable amount of persuasion to get him out of bed to help. Strangely, some people take this as a picture of persistent prayer—of continuing to pray until God answers—but, of course, it really draws the contrast between an earthly father and the heavenly Father. With the heavenly Father it is simply, "Ask, and it will be given you; seek, and you will find; knock, and it will be opened to you." Our God is always accessible. So I can turn to him in prayer at any time and in any place—in a bus, on a train, walking down the street, working in the kitchen, lying in bed, sitting at my desk, changing a car tire, or lining up at the supermarket checkout counter.

A loving richness

Luke 11 encourages us further. The way in which an earthly father responds to requests is not likely to be perverse or malicious—giving a serpent instead of a fish, or a scorpion instead of an egg. We usually take great care in selecting gifts for birthdays and Christmas for those we love. We trudge around the stores with our lists and compare the different brands available, trying to get the item most suitable to a particular person. The amateur photographer wants some special new lens, the mechanically-minded four-year-old wants something with which he can *make things,* the older friend just retiring from work may want a really comfortable garden chair, the teenager wants the record that "everybody else has" and so on down the list. Love takes care to respond to the individual need.

We have already seen from our discussion of the foundations of prayer that we cannot treat God like a Santa Claus who doles out whatever our selfishness demands. However, we *can* trust him to give the best gifts. As Jesus said, even sinful human fathers do quite well in choosing good gifts for their children. How much more is this true of our heavenly Father, who is perfect and untainted by sin and whose gifts and blessings come through the gracious agency of the Holy Spirit. The parallel passage in Matthew 7:11 says: "How much more will your Father who is in heaven give good things to those who ask him." The whole context is of gifts given in answer to prayer (not just of the first-time gift of the Holy Spirit). We see that the readiness of our Father to answer prayer is matched by his discernment and loving wisdom. He wants the best for us as his children and that best will be decided in terms of his will and purposes, not in feeding our selfish desires. He responds to us out of a love that wants the best for us.

As we bring our requests to him we need to be conscious of our fallibility, our limited vision, and our sinfulness and trust him to know how best to answer. S. D. Gordon wrote: "If God were to say to me, 'I want to give you a special love-gift—what would you like?' I would say, 'Dear God *you* choose.' He knows what I would most enjoy and he would choose something finer than I would think." That deliberate trust on our part is an expression of our submission as his children and our thankfulness that we can come to him, giving ourselves and our needs into the security of his love as our heavenly Father.

CHAPTER   11

APPROACHING GOD AS BRIDE TO BRIDEGROOM

AS WE CONTINUE IN THE CHRISTIAN LIFE we discover a deepening closeness to our Lord as expressed in John 15:4, 9: "As the Father has loved me, so have I loved you, abide in my love." "Abide in me and I in you." This is the language of intimacy, of union, of love.

Love needs time. She sat down in the row in front of mine just as the lecture began. Her flaxen hair bounced as she laughed. There was something special about her. A few months later I went on a mission in Leeds and the same girl was part of the mission team. Two actresses were attracted to Christ during that mission, but did not come to faith. They worked in London and so "the girl" and I were asked to follow them up. We took them to a Crusade meeting where they trusted Christ. But another "follow-up" was developing! At first I could not believe that this attractive girl could be interested in me. My college friends teased me about her. At last, I plucked up courage and invited her to tea. She said "Yes." She responded again when I asked her out. We walked in the Kentish countryside and prayed in the village church at Ide Hill. We loved to be together. Eventually I proposed—on the unromantic railway platform of Penge West Station! Since our wedding we have spent even more time together!

Love needs time. Even if it is "love at first sight," the enrichment of love is never instant. If I had said to Myrtle: "I can spare you five minutes on Monday, I'm too busy on Tuesday, maybe ten minutes on Wednesday if I'm not too tired, I might squeeze in fifteen minutes on Thursday, though Friday is unlikely, Saturday should be all right for an hour or two, depending on what's on TV, and a couple of hours on Sunday (sorry if I get there late)," there would not have been much enrichment of love. Love in courtship or marriage, and love in friendship, needs time spent together getting to know one another.

Delight or drudgery?
So it is in our love relationship with Jesus. It may begin with "love at first sight" or a gradual growing attachment, but enrichment of that love needs a lifetime—and beyond! When a girl is in love she is excited. "I'll be seeing Peter today!" There is anticipation. The time is not begrudged. Is that how we love the Lord? Is time spent with him a burden, a nuisance, something we have to fit in? Or is it anticipated with delight? If our daily times of devotion and prayer have become dry or difficult or mere discipline, might it be that we have stopped seeing those times as opportunities to be with *him*?

The Bible speaks of Jesus as the Bridegroom and we, his Church, as the bride. The newly-married need to learn to "give and take." There is much to discover about one another. A friend of mine did everything possible to avoid letting the hotel know that he and his wife were on their honeymoon, until the porter said: "Would you like morning tea, sir?" He turned to his new wife and was asking her "Do you like . . ." when the words froze on his lips! We learn each other's preferences—what sort of drink with dinner, scenic or beach holidays, mustard or horseradish with ham, cloves or cinnamon in apple pie, the use of money, standards of hospitality, what brings joy or pain.

But it is completely different in our relationship with Jesus. He is perfect. He does not need to adjust to us, he already knows us through and through. "Christ loved the church and gave himself up for her [us], that he might sanctify her [us], having cleansed her [us] by the washing of water with the word, that he might present the church to himself in splendor, without spot or wrinkle or any such thing, that she [we] might be holy and without blemish." (Eph. 5:25-27). Christ wants us to press on towards perfection. He wants us to be lovelier and lovelier as people —growing in his grace and producing the fruit of the Spirit. The adaptation is entirely on our side. *We* are to adapt to *Christ*.

He meets our imperfect love with his: "If a man loves me, he will keep my word, and my Father will love him, and we will come to him and make our home with him" (John 14:23). There are times when that love overwhelms us, when it is a mountain-top experience, or when we want to cry with wonder as we are touched by his loving action, kindness, or thoughtfulness. Christianity is a love affair. We will want to respond to that love. At times we will want to break our alabaster box of sacrificial devotion, or to respond in praise and worship, or in going, serving, caring, daring for him. Such love needs time—time alone, time apart. Such time is vital to every Christian and especially to those who lead or minister to others. As Spurgeon said to ministers: "If you become lax in sacred devotion not only will you need to be pitied but your people also, and the day cometh in which you will need to be ashamed and confounded." The danger of the Christian minister is to "be too busy to pray" just when he needs to pray *more*. William Wilberforce wrote: "I must secure more time for private devotions. I have been living far too public for me. The shortening of the devotions starves the soul; it grows lean and faint." It has been said that if we're too busy to pray, we're too busy.

The fundamental question is: "Do we *want* to change? Do we *want* to grow more like Christ?" For a few months during the Second World War, I was evacuated from London to a village in Leicestershire. I was a choirboy at home, so joined the choir of that village's church. The choirmaster decided that some of our voices could benefit from some extra choral training. He was persuasive and told us to come to his house on the Wednesday evening at 7 P.M. That was also the last night that a certain film about a haunted house was being shown at the local cinema. We wanted to see it. We went to the choirmaster's house with dragging feet. Hope rose when we found he was not back from a meeting. We waited, looking at the clock. When he did not come we took courage in both hands and spoke to his wife: "He'll be tired when he gets in. He'll need to eat. He won't feel like teaching us..." She let us go and we ran as fast as we could. At a road junction we spied the choirmaster walking towards us in the dark. We ran faster, in the other direction. We saw the film. It wasn't worth the effort!

The key to our feelings about the incident was that we did not particularly *want* to have our voices improved. And the key to our spending time in personal devotion lies in our desire. Do I *want* the Master Gardener to prune this branch of the vine? Do I *want* to be strengthened with might by his Spirit? Do I *want* to know more of his love? Do I *want* to be filled with all the fullness of God? Do I *want* to be more holy, more worthy of the Bridegroom? If so, I will ensure that I have time apart with my Lord, day by day, and at other special times.

The daily quiet time

First, let's be practical about spending time with him "day by day." Jesus said: "When you pray, go into your room and shut the door and pray to your Father who is in secret" (Matt. 6:6). The primary reason for his saying this was to avoid the pitfall of praying for appearance. However, the principle of being alone is a good one. If we have our own room there is no problem, but not everyone is so privileged. Is there anywhere for us to get away? If not, can we shut out distractions of noise, putting hands over our ears? Kneeling is a helpful posture for many. Certainly Jesus knelt down (Luke 22:41); there are numerous references to kneeling in the Acts of the Apostles; Paul said "I bow my knees," in Ephesians 3:14. But kneeling may be unhelpful. Our body posture needs to allow our spirit to commune with the Lord, and that may mean that we keep moving, walking up and down the room, if sleepiness threatens. And what about atmosphere? Are you affected by your surroundings? At college some students do nothing about their rooms, leaving them basic and "cold." It doesn't bother them at all. Others make their rooms "friendly" with cozy furnishings and pictures. It *matters* to them. If possible, I like to pray in a "friendly" environment surrounded by the beauty of the Lord's creation. The growth of my love-relationship with the Lord is helped by lovely surroundings though it *can* be as real in the midst of the sordidness and clamor of the inner city.

When should we have a quiet time? When we say we cannot get up to pray we may be deceiving ourselves. Thousands of people get up in time to jog, to decorate their faces, to eat. Why not to pray? A motto in our church office asks "Is there life before breakfast?" But if you find the morning impossible for personal devotions, at least greet the Lord! For many it is better to be alone with the Lord later in the day—at lunchtime or on the way home from work, at the end of the day. If you love him, and want to love him more, you will not have to "find" time or "make" time—it will be a priority in your day.

Special times
Second, let's be practical about the special times to spend with God. We do not know whether Jesus went apart every day. We assume so, because he walked so closely with his Father. However, we *do* know that he had some special times apart, particularly after days of pressure, when the crowds pressed upon him as in Mark 1 and 3. When choosing the Twelve he spent the whole night in prayer. After the mission of the disciples and John's beheading he went apart; before turning towards Jerusalem he went up to the Mount of Transfiguration; before the Cross he went to Gethsemane. If Jesus needed to do this, how much more do we need to get away, occasionally or regularly? We may call it a "retreat" and make it at least an annual break, a time of re-evaluation. Alan Stibbs, the beloved expositor and lecturer, used to speak of the "one decisive Lent" of his life when he sorted out God's way forward for him. Like Jesus, we may need to balance these special times away against the times of pressure or new challenges.

The benefit of these times away is that we can relax and unwind. The telephone, the urgent requests, the decision-making, the non-stop whirl of activity—all are left behind. After the dust has settled, we will begin to experience the "restoration of the soul" spoken of in Psalm 23—the atmosphere of the "still waters" and "green pastures." It can be enormously helpful to spend such times in surroundings of beauty. Some of the most glorious times of restoration for me have been in the mountains of Switzerland. Once, after a time of particular pressure, some Christian friends paid for my wife and me to have a short "luxury" holiday. We went first class on the train to Cornwall and over by helicopter to the Scilly Isles. The next four days were spent in the beauty of the islands, going out in boats morning and afternoon, staying at a lovely hotel overlooking the sea. Our souls were restored. Of course, these are very special experiences. There are nearer places of beauty and, for some, an exposure to beauty in music and art is restorative. Not that such beauty is sufficient in itself, but it warms the soul and provides an atmosphere in which we may find it easier to be restored in our love-relationship with Christ. A stimulating Christian book may be an instrument of blessing, or simply meditating on the Scriptures, or just digesting what one has heard and read over recent months. And we need time to simply converse with the Lord.

Such times are also necessary for checking our navigation —of setting the course of our lives by deciding what is important and what is secondary. In Mark 1 Jesus did not return to the crowd at Peter's house but altered his course: "I must go to other cities also." For us the rush and activity of life often mean that we can't see the forest for the trees. We get hurt by comments or criticisms but by getting away we can see them in perspective—realizing that we are, ultimately, answerable to the Lord and not to man for our life. When others tell us that they are praying for us to be like someone else and have their gifts (or when we wish this ourselves) we need to stand back and realize that we are called to run the race set before *us* and not before someone else. Vision and direction can be wonderfully renewed for us by such times apart and our eyes lifted beyond and above the task to Jesus himself.

Time for a refill
Sometimes we need the refilling of the Holy Spirit. This should be our daily desire, but we will particularly pray for his refilling after times of special tiredness and busyness,

and as we face what lies ahead. What a demonstration of this is seen in Acts 4:31, where the bruised and battered disciples throw themselves on their sovereign Lord and seek the refilling of the Spirit in order to speak the Word of God with boldness! In 1 Corinthians 12:13 we are told that "by one Spirit we were all baptized into one body"—the initiatory act of the Spirit—but then, "and were made to drink of one Spirit." In the physical realm, fluids must be taken day by day—we cannot drink enough water to last us a month. So in Christ we need to drink of the Spirit day by day and in the special times apart we need particular refilling to overcome our spiritual dehydration, desiring to grow in the fruit of the Spirit and seeking his gifting for the tasks ahead. We do not want simply to *feel* renewed; we want to in actuality *be* restored, renewed, refilled, and ready to go on for our Lord, being more fruitful in his service and deepened in the privilege of abiding in him and he in us —the privilege of the supreme love-relationship, into which he brought us and which continues for ever.

Let Charles Wesley express our prayer and hope:

Finish then thy new creation
Pure and spotless let us be:
Let us see thy great salvation
Perfectly retored in thee.

Changed from glory into glory,
Till in heaven we take our place;
Till we cast our crowns before thee,
Lost in wonder, love and praise.

3
INTERCESSION

CHAPTER 12

PRAYING
IN THE
BATTLE

THE BIGGEST SURPRISE MOST OF US WILL HAVE when we get to heaven will be to see, from a wholly new perspective, the scope and intensity of the spiritual battle. So often we are like soldiers in a battle who are told that the enemy is attacking forcibly, but because we cannot see him we do little about it and so we are over-run and defeated.

Ephesians 6:18-20 is a key passage for understanding the scope of intercession. "Pray at all times in the Spirit, with all prayer and supplication. To that end keep alert with all perseverance, making supplication for all the saints, and also for me, that utterance may be given me in opening my mouth boldly to proclaim the mystery of the gospel." The passage forms the basis for most of this section of the book. But notice its context; from verse 10 on it is the context of *battle*—being strong in the Lord, putting on the whole armor of God, standing against the wiles of the devil, contending against the spiritual hosts of wickedness.

You can win the spiritual battle only with the right weapons. You can't interrupt a radio-wave with a flyswatter; you can't stop a bullet with a plastic raincoat; you can't block a laser beam with a piece of cardboard; and you can't disarm the Evil One without spiritual armor and the weapons of the Word and prayer, or as the old English put it, "the weapon of all-prayer." Churches and Christian groups which do not see the necessity of intercessory prayer might as well close their doors at once—they will be defeated.

In prayer we take the spiritual battle seriously and "mean business" with the Lord of all power and might. There are five characteristics of real prayer (or "prayer in the Spirit," as Ephesians 6:18 expresses it).

Accurate intercession

Vague, waffling prayer is a waste of time and breath. To be effective, prayer must be on target. Here the Spirit is ready to help and direct us. As Romans 8:26 puts it: "The Spirit helps us in our weakness; for we do not know how to pray as we ought, but the Spirit himself intercedes for us with sighs too deep for words." That can be our experience in personal intercession when a deep burden of the Spirit comes upon us, and prompts us to lift that burden to the Lord. Similarly, in corporate intercession, when a topic suddenly comes "on fire," the Spirit will burden us as a group for a person or an event, and all other topics will be temporarily dropped as we concentrate on that one thing. As James Montgomery's hymn puts it: "Prayer is the soul's sincere desire, uttered or unexpressed, the motion of a hidden fire that trembles in the breast."

The Spirit can help us to focus on one aspect of a mission enterprise 10,000 miles away, burdening us with the right request for that moment; or he can motivate our hearts at any time of day or night to pray, and only after many months do we learn how that prayer fitted into God's plan and how we were part of a vital prayer force in that intense spiritual battle. How often we will learn from a missionary (or someone else serving God) that he was conscious of being supported in a special way, given the right words to speak in a difficult moment, or delivered from danger, at the exact time we were burdened to pray.

As we intercede through our prayer lists, individually or with others, let us keep alert to the Spirit's prompting that we may be accurate in prayer.

Fervent intercession
James 5:16-18 tells us "The prayer of a righteous man has great power in its effects. Elijah was a man of like nature with ourselves and he prayed fervently that it might not rain, and for three years and six months it did not rain on the earth. Then he prayed again and the heaven gave rain and the earth brought forth its fruit." Some praying! What does "fervently" mean? Many people assume that fervency implies a special intensity. Prayer expressed with deep emotion is regarded by them as the only effective prayer and straightforward speaking to God is dismissed as not fervent enough. This is an inaccurate interpretation and an unhelpful viewpoint. Literally, the Greek here says "with prayer he prayed." Nothing is said about a trembling voice, but the obvious meaning is that he meant business with God —his prayer was real and from the heart. He really *prayed*.

When we come to pray, it must not be empty words or an outward facade. Prayer in a service or a prayer gathering which seems to be meant more for the human hearers than for God to hear is off-center, like the prayer described as "the most eloquent prayer ever offered to a Boston congregation." Prayer is to God, from the heart, with reality. This is fervency, and prayer without such fervency is not prayer. The disciples found themselves helpless in dealing with the demoniac boy in Mark 9:29;. Was it because they "used" prayer as a formula for healing but did not really come in fervent heart-prayer to God? Is this why Jesus warned "this kind cannot be driven out by anything but prayer (and fasting)"?

I need to ask myself: "Is my interceding always fervent? Or do I let my prayers become a recital, a routine rather than a genuine crying out to the Lord?" Do our prayer gatherings seek to maintain this God-centered, God-dependent fervency?

Expectant intercession

James 1:6 tells us to "Ask in faith, with no doubting, for he who doubts is like a wave of the sea that is driven and tossed by the wind. For that person must not suppose that a double-minded man, unstable in all his ways, will receive anything from the Lord."

Our expectancy is, of course, subject to the purposes and ways of God, but it is still a real mark of our praying, not least because God is always *able* to do more than we ask or think. This rules out of order the sort of tentative praying that mentions a matter because God *might* want to do something about it, but we can't see how and we don't really expect an answer—and so we don't get one!

On the other hand, submitting our requests to the will and plans of God will protect us from the immature, mechanical view of this phrase "Ask in faith" which one sometimes hears: "I pray in faith for my parents, and all my brothers and sisters—that they may all be converted, by the end of the week."

Expectancy, coupled with the humble "Your will be done, O Lord," is a mark of real prayer. When we come to special evangelistic services in our churches it is not much use for us to pray without expectancy. We must learn to pray "on target" for spiritual blindness to be removed, for power in testimony and the ministry of the Word and for the Holy Spirit to be moving among us. We must expect God to bring *his* results, which may be to move a lot of people a step nearer the Kingdom, rather than a few people actually coming to Christ. Expect, and on that occasion trust the Lord to know what is best.

Expectancy can also be a growing conviction. We may face up to a venture for the Lord, some specific challenge to prayer. As we pray—over a period of weeks or months —we begin to sense that "the Lord is in this." When there are encouraging signs of our being in line with his will, our expectancy increases and we begin to have the kind of faith in God that believes mountains can be removed (Mark 11:23-24).

Earnest intercession
When Peter was in prison "earnest prayer for him was made to God by the church" (Acts 12:5). What does "earnest" mean? Again, some people put it in the emotion-in-the-voice category, but the original word actually has the sense of laying hands on someone and thus identifying with them. So, as the group of Christians prayed for Peter they identified with him, lifting him up to the Lord together with love, urgency, and deep oneness. When a person in special need is with us in a prayer gathering some of us may lay hands on his head, as a representation of the group's identification with him and an outward sign of our inward "earnestness" in prayer for him. In the same way, in our personal intercessions, it is good to try and identify with the person for whom we are praying—with what they must be feeling and facing.

But our earnestness must be also towards God. Jesus in Gethsemane showed this. As Luke 22:44 records it: "And being in an agony he prayed more *earnestly*; and his sweat became like great drops of blood falling down upon the ground." Here, in a sense, Jesus was laying hands on his Father, deeply identifying with the Father's will, in spite of the enormous burden as he anticipated Calvary. There are

those who seem specially called to be deep intercessors—
warriors of prayer—with that ability to come earnestly to
the Lord. There are also times when God calls us to spend
days or nights in prayer together as a church or as groups
(as Jesus did before choosing the Twelve). Those who have
shared in extended times of concentrated prayer like this
know how, after a while, the reality of meeting with the
Lord seems to deepen and prayer itself takes on the rich
dimension of earnestness.

Persistent intercession
The fifth mark of real prayer comes from Ephesians 6:18
itself: "Keep alert with all perseverance." We often have to
persevere in prayer *because we cannot see* what is happening
in the spiritual realm. Daniel 10 is an example of this. Only
after Daniel had spent three weeks of prayer and fasting
did the heavenly messenger tell him that his prayer was
heard from the beginning but the answer was delayed because "the prince of the kingdom of Persia withstood me
twenty-one days."

We may never fully understand how effective our
prayers are in the spiritual battle, nor how our prayers
affect God's will and action. But it is clear from Scripture
that prayer does "change things," and this is why we must
press on in persevering prayer—perhaps for many years—
when we know that the matter has been laid on our hearts
by the Holy Spirit. We must trust God's timing.

Here is someone who has prayed for forty years for his
son to come to faith and dies without seeing the answer.
Then the son is actually brought to Christ through his
father's funeral! Here is a small group of Christians in an
area that seems dead spiritually. The ministers of the local
churches seem to have grown cold spiritually. The flame of
the gospel seems almost extinguished. But the group re-
solves to pray and persevere. Then, the impossible happens. A new minister is appointed who is spiritually alive

and the Kingdom of God begins to grow in that area. Here are the multitudes who persevere in prayer for the Muslim world, or for the Jews, or for other religious groups that seem very resistant to the gospel. The burden is laid on their hearts to pray. How much perseverance they must have. Here is another group facing a new venture for Christ. Their expectancy has grown and they are sure they are in the Lord's will but the obstacles come, one by one, and they have to pray for God's solution and over-ruling time and time again. The battle continues down to the wire and they must not grow tired. They have been called to persevering prayer.

Martin Luther encourages us by saying, "To pray diligently is more than half the task." We may not always understand the how and the why of prayer but two things *are* clear—the disaster of no-prayer and the power of real prayer. We wrestle against the forces of spiritual darkness, but we wrestle in the power of God as we join in "battle prayer" with accuracy, fervency, expectancy, earnestness and perseverance. "Pray at all times in the Spirit, with all prayer and supplication."

CHAPTER 13

PRAYING
AT ALL
TIMES

THERE ARE MANY OPPORTUNITIES AND AVENUES for intercessory prayer. Let us think our way through a number of
them:

The spontaneous breath of prayer
The habit of lifting our hearts in intercession sponta-
neously, at any time of day or night, is a valuable way of
spreading the coverage of prayer. When we are about to
write a letter or make a telephone call, can we pause and lift
what we write or say to the Lord? When we are about to
have an interview with a prospective employer, or we ourselves are about to do the interviewing, can we pause to
pray? When we are starting a journey, perhaps setting off
on a family vacation, can we pause to pray? When we are
sitting in a bus or a subway train, can our eyes go around

the bus or train praying for our fellow-passengers? When we are crammed into an elevator on its way to the twenty-fifth floor, can we pray for the other people going up? When we are reading the newspaper, listening to the news on the radio or on television, can we turn our minds to God in prayer, lifting up to him those with colossal responsibility in leadership or people caught in some disaster or the relatives of people killed in a plane crash? Once we learn the habit of breathing prayer, our intercession becomes limitless.

Personal intercession

Interceding alone does not seem as easily practicable as we would like to think. Some years ago I was asked to write a paper on "Spirituality" for a group of ministers. I did some practical research by means of anonymous questionnaires and in interviewing small groups of Christians who would be honest with me about their spiritual lives. I found that the amount of time spent in intercession by the ministers was far less than I would have imagined. Then, in talking with a group of outstanding Christian laymen, all influential leaders in the local church, I was staggered to find that though all of them kept a regular time each day for devotional prayer, approaching God for the new day, *none* of them had daily times of intercession for others. It is not possible to assess how widespread is this state of affairs, but I suspect it may be far more general than we would like to believe.

The reason seems to be partly a matter of time, partly because intercessory prayer is easier in a group (and all the laymen I spoke to were regular intercessors at the church prayer gathering), and partly a matter of system. It may be that the burden of personal intercession is to be on those who have more time—the elderly or those laid aside with illness. Many retired people are faithful intercessors and I am often amazed by (though thankful for) the care with which they support my ministry and the life of the Church at home and abroad. I know I cannot match that but it does not free me from intercessory responsibility. There are times when we can give ourselves more fully to intercession, and in a recent time in the hospital for an operation I found great joy in being able to intercede without the usual time limitation. Yet I must find time in my normal daily life. Intercession may be separate from my devotional approach to God or the two may come together.

Then, what about a system? Though we may need no system to pray daily for our family, ourselves, and others who are close to us (we carry them so close to our hearts), we may find it difficult to be fresh in prayer. The suggestion made earlier in the book (chapter 7 on "Worship") that we take a fresh thought from our reading of the Scriptures and use it in prayer can be a solution. It is, of course, an idea we can carry into all our intercession that day.

If for instance, the text "You will keep him in perfect peace whose mind is stayed on you" has blessed our hearts that morning, then we could pray for that staying of the mind on the Lord and its consequent peace for ourselves, members of our family, colleagues, missionaries, and so on. The next day the Word to our hearts might emphasize spiritual growth, and that could be our particular prayer concern for ourselves and others. Thus each day our regular praying is fresh and refreshing.

Beyond our immediate family and friends, some system is necessary if we are to cover the multiple needs for prayer. Here a loose-leaf notebook is a practical help. The first page could be for daily prayer, though it is doubtful whether we need a list, as these people and concerns will naturally be on our hearts. However, we might find it helpful to write down certain prayers which are helpful to us.

Next we need to organize the objects of our prayer for the week. We must decide whether to make this a seven-day coverage or perhaps a six- or five-day coverage, leaving out

Saturday and/or when we gather with other Christians for worship and instruction. Some will say that Sunday is *the* day for intercession as they have more time. Work that out in your own way! Some may omit Saturday because it is a "day off."

Once we have decided on the days to pray, we must decide how to use them. Personally, I find it difficult to move instantly from praying, say, for South America, to praying for the elderly of my own parish, and then for next week's mission in the inner city. For me it was a break-through when I "went thematic." Each day was assigned its own theme for intercession—Monday for all those who work with me in the local church program, and for every section of that church's life; Tuesday for all missionaries and world missions, as well as world leaders; Wednesday for the wider range of my family, my friends, people for whom I have a particular spiritual responsibility, and for all new Christians; Thursday for the wide range of my friends and acquaintances in Christian ministry or in "secular" occupations, with opportunities for effective influence for Christ; Friday for the spectrum of Christian organizations involved in evangelism, outreach, social work, relief of world need, the arts and so on; Saturday, for all the activities on Sunday. The liberty this gave me was that if, on a particular day, I felt I could not face a long list of topics and names, I could still give myself freely to praying on the theme of that day, open to the Spirit's leading. It meant too that some names or needs on the lists would become special targets for prayer as the Spirit touched my heart. It is a system that has never become stale for me though I have used it for many years. You can adapt such a prayer pattern to your own outreach and interest. As well as following this weekly pattern, we should obviously pray each day for the particular events of that day in our church's program—for the classes of new believers, youth groups and so on.

I also use the monthly church diary of our parish. This

lists our missionaries and world mission projects on one side of the page across the thirty days and a detailed breakdown of our church's activities and its leaders on the other side. This helps to balance our prayer interest between the local and the worldwide work of God. To this monthly list can be added the names of people for whom we want to pray whom we cannot "handle" in the scope of weekly prayer.

Clearly we cannot pray for everyone and every need we see or hear about. Specific needs will be particularly on our hearts for prayer and in that framework we should try to keep our praying informed. It would be impossible to do that for the whole world. The same selectivity is obviously necessary over the whole panorama of prayer.

One other page we may add to our notebook is for prayer for short-term needs—specific events, or crises or opportunities or exams. This page requires frequent updating, but it does help us to fulfill our promises often so readily made, to pray for people when they ask us to do so.

Intercession in twos and threes
The promise of the Lord in Matthew 18:19 is that "if two of you agree on earth about anything they ask, it will be done for them by my Father in heaven. For where two or three are gathered in my name, there am I in the midst of them." Why should prayer in twos and threes be more effective? Perhaps because of the Lord's promised presence when we are together, we can sense more accurately when we are praying "on target." It is true that for many Christians, intercessory prayer occurs more normally and naturally in such a group of two or three than alone. Some married couples pray regularly in this way. So do close friends, especially if they are sharing a house or apartment. At my theological college we had a "prayer partnership" plan. We joined in prayer voluntarily with a different fellow-student each week, in fellowship and prayer. Some weeks it meant praying with people I seemed to have nothing in common

with, but often, as we met together to pray, real understanding and friendship developed. It seems natural for us
as Christian friends to pray together before visiting a sick
person in a hospital or at home, or after discussing a personal problem. We may want to pray together briefly following a counselling session, or after spending an evening
of fellowship together in a home, or even before saying
goodbye on a street corner! When Paul said farewell to the
Ephesian elders in Acts 20:36, they all kneeled, prayed,
cried, and embraced. How spontaneous and fitting that
seems, in the context of Christian family love!

Intercession in the body—the prayer gathering
I can understand the hesitancy of some people about open
prayer gatherings, regarding them as "super-spiritual"
events. I had the same feelings when I was a youth. Then
one morning on the way to work I made a very careless
mistake. The leader of our Youth Group said: "See you at
the P.M. on Saturday, Michael?" I am never very good at
initials, especially early in the morning, and I mistook "P.M."
for "Y.F." (Youth Fellowship). I said "Yes," without thinking, then I realized what I had said. *P.M. stood for prayer
meeting*! My youthful pride conflicted with my fear. Pride
won and I turned up for the prayer meeting. Only two
others were there. We knelt in the front room of the house,
each one at a chair. Mine was a deep blue velvet-covered
armchair. I remember it vividly! The other two (girls)
prayed fluently and at length. Then there was a long silence
while the sweat broke out on my forehead and streamed
down my face, on to the blue velvet! Eventually I stuttered
out some sort of prayer. Mercifully this exposure to a
prayer meeting did not frighten me off for life, but it did
make me ask myself why I should get into such a lather
about praying to God aloud, as I had no difficulty praying
in silence nor talking aloud to others about anything and
everything! If you are a new Christian, don't avoid the

prayer gathering. (It will usually be much larger than three and you won't usually be embarrassed; others will pray if you are silent.) It will widen the scope of your praying. You will learn from others and be helped to pray for many people and needs, agreeing in your mind with the one leading in prayer. You may find it helpful to write out a prayer and to "break the ice" of opening your mouth in a prayer gathering by reading it aloud. To move on to extempore praying, you will need to have the Lord firmly at the center of your thoughts, and forget about the other people present (does it really matter what they think?). If some others use "thou," "wast," "hath," and so on, don't copy them. Use today's English. There's no special holiness about Elizabethan language and it can get you in a tangle. God expects us to pray straight forwardly and from the heart. For most of us that will be in our everyday language and without undue length.

The prayer gathering is of key importance in the life of any church. It should never be an option or thought of as just one event among many. It must have the best night of the week and nothing else should conflict with it in the church's program on that night. In All Souls it is every other Tuesday. We have established a pattern of meeting all together on one Tuesday and then in fellowship groups on the next. The fellowship groups concentrate on Bible study and sharing personal prayer needs, as well as on friendship and support. The prayer gathering concentrates on praise and prayer, particularly for the church's work and for world missions. All leaders are expected to be at the prayer gathering and to give it top priority, and the entire church family is urged to be present.

The pattern of our meeting has been carefully worked out. Before the actual gathering, there is an opportunity to eat together or have coffee. Then, for the meeting itself, the seating is set as closely as possible in concentric circles to aid audibility and create a sense of being together with Christ at the center. We begin with worship, then move into praise and thanksgiving. We ask that praises should be brief—phrases or sentences but not paragraphs. This enables a good number of people to share in thanking and praising God. Normally we remain standing, and sing to start and end this section.

Then we may have a brief thought from the Scriptures —a keynote to focus our praying. This is followed by a collated list of prayer needs and topics. Time is taken to explain these needs so that we can later be "agreed" in prayer for them. Sometimes we pray first for an urgent or special need. Often different leaders or members will mention briefly the needs of their group or of a friend. In the case of prayer for healing we may ask the individual to come into the center so that we can hear from him or her firsthand and lay on hands as we pray. Around the room the needs are then taken up in prayer. We encourage "conversational" prayer, that is, spending a short time on a topic, with several prayers for it or prayers that lead naturally to a similar need. We discourage lengthy praying. At times a particular theme seems to come "on fire" and the Spirit leads us to concentrate at length on it. Quite often we have a time at the end of this section when we say a name of a person, mentioning a need or an event, without introductions or endings to the prayer. This is particularly helpful for those who may panic at framing a longer prayer. We often then pray silently for those next to us, so that everyone present is prayed for.

A time of prayer in small groups usually follows, but not always. We turn our chairs into circles of five or six and either pray for one or two special topics, such as the next evangelistic service, or for needs of people in the group. It is not over-long, so as to avoid embarrassment to those not able to articulate prayers. We bring it to an end with the piano being played to introduce a hymn.

The final section is normally on world missions. If we

have a missionary at home on furlough we will obviously focus this time on him, or her, and the work in which he is involved. At other times we will cover a particular area of the world, or concentrate on a work of outreach or relief. We end with a hymn followed by quite a number of informal announcements in a family atmosphere, after which people stay on to meet, talk, and share fellowship. The meeting itself lasts about one-and-a-half hours. It is the hub of our life and work at All Souls.

Intercession in the Body—in church services

Is the intercessory part of a service the "low" part for us, the time when our mind wanders? Is it too formal in liturgical services and too world-roving in non-liturgical services? It certainly ought to be a vital part of the service, involving the whole congregation in "agreement" in prayer. This could be helped by having different leaders who make very careful preparation by so fitting into the theme of the church service that the prayers have a fresh perspective or thrust each week, by congregational response after each item of prayer, by extempore prayer from the congregation if the church is fairly small, or by asking several people to lead in prayer from the congregation. An overhead projector showing a map or a drawing can focus our prayer concentration. The occasional visual prayer when we project color slides and pray for the need portrayed by each one, can be refreshing. To a large extent the key to freshness and relevance lies with the person leading and the time and thought he gives to this important part of the service, but the rest of the congregation must make it their conscious resolve not just to listen, but to pray.

Special times of prayer

The New Testament gives us several examples of special gatherings for prayer in the church, as in the setting apart of Saul and Barnabas, or for Peter in prison. When as a church, or a Christian group, we face special challenges, we should meet them with special prayer. This will be true in a venture of faith such as a building project, or during a time of concentrated opposition to the gospel in our area, or as we have a mission or are called on to make some big decision. We may call the church together for an evening of prayer, a day of prayer, or a night of prayer. We may arrange a series of special gatherings and ask those who cannot come to pray wherever they are at that time (for example, in the early morning).

S.O.S. prayer
Sometimes there are urgent prayers that cannot wait for a meeting to be arranged. There may be a call from a member of a fellowship or part of the church's extended family elsewhere in the country or overseas. Often it will be about a sudden illness, a matter of life-and-death;, or some devastating emotional crisis or threat. At times like these we will often telephone various friends and fellow-members of the church, asking them for S.O.S. prayer. Separately (and together when possible) the fellowship has to swing into action, lifting the person or persons onto the stretcher of prayer and bringing them to the feet of the Lord. It is literally a matter of "stop—and pray."

Special support
When a friend is facing a tough day or a tough week, an exam, an interview, a difficult decision, an operation, or a speaking engagement, we need to keep reminding ourselves to lift them to the Lord through the day or through the week. I am grateful to my wife for praying when I am speaking, even when I am in a different time-zone of the world, and I am equally grateful to the numerous other members of the church who do the same. It is a privilege of Christian fellowship to receive and give this special prayer support.

Seeing a spiritual need

When we see a *material* need in one of our brothers or sisters we are to meet it by action and giving, if possible. When we see a *spiritual* need we should meet it with action and praying. 1 John 5:16 tells us, "If any one sees his brother committing what is not a mortal sin, he will ask and God will give him life . . . ." Older Christians can often see the dangers facing younger Christians. Youth has its own self-confidence but older Christians were once young too, and they have remarkable memories! They can see the errors of judgment in decisions being made and know the possible consequences. They may feel hesitant about giving their advice, but they can pray. Peter "couldn't be told" about his impending failure and denial, so Jesus prayed for him that his faith would not fail. Such spiritual alertness and prayerfulness need not be confined to the older members—it is part of real Christian fellowship and love for us all—and the effects of such prayer may have eternal consequences.

CHAPTER 14

PRAYING FOR "THE SAINTS"

EPHESIANS 6:18 SPEAKS OF "MAKING SUPPLICATION for all the saints." The description "saints" as applied to all those who belong to God is used more than sixty times in the New Testament. The less exact modern usage—as in, "I'm no saint,"—has devalued the biblical concept of "the Lord's people," those who belong to his family for ever, his saints. Paul's command to pray "for all the saints" calls us to the responsibility of special prayer support for the whole of the Lord's family here on earth and particularly for all whom we know personally in it. This love and prayer-care for fellow believers is well demonstrated by Paul himself. He writes, for instance, to the Thessalonians: "We give thanks to God always for you all, constantly mentioning you in our prayers."

For us this will mean praying for fellow-members of our

church or Christian groups and Christians we know anywhere in the world. We will want to include most of them
in our monthly prayer list so that we can pray specifically
and systematically for them, but we will also want to lift
some to the Lord whenever we think of them. What do we
pray? A quick "Bless Pat," or "Bless Jim"? Or is there more
to it? There are three aspects of prayer for fellow-Christians in the New Testament which may guide us in our
praying for them—but, we are also saints through faith in
Christ, and we should pray the same for ourselves.

Prayer for spiritual well-being
It is natural to pray first for our own or our fellow-Christians' safety, well-being, health, or success. However, if we
read through the prayers of the New Testament we find
them overwhelmingly concerned with the spiritual growth
of believers. Spiritual well-being must be our prayer
priority.

Ephesians 3:14-19 gives us a model for such prayer. It
is a magnificent expression of heartfelt praying for the
Ephesians to know increasing spiritual power, in terms of
the riches of God's glory rather than mere human expectation. How much we need to pray like this! Even though we
have been born anew by the Holy Spirit, brought into a
spiritual dimension of living, we can so easily grow content
with mediocre spiritual standards, lacking boldness in witnessing, and failing to maintain victory in the fight against
"the world, the flesh and the devil." In our own strength
we will fail. Only by the increasing power of the Holy Spirit
can we keep growing and gaining in the spiritual realm.

Paul then prays that "Christ may dwell in your hearts
through faith." The Holy Spirit glorifies Christ. It follows
that a person full of the Holy Spirit will be Christ-centered
rather than Spirit-centered. As the Holy Spirit strengthens
us, we find ourselves closer to Christ, saying, with Paul, "I
can do all things in Christ who strengthens me." While the

letter to the Philippians is full of Christ it hardly mentions the Holy Spirit. Yet Paul is clearly filled with the Holy Spirit. Again, it is the Spirit who opens up to us what Christ means when he tells us "Abide in me and I in you."

Paul's prayer is concerned next with the fruit of Christian character, that his friends in Ephesus will be rooted and grounded in love—knowing the deep security of the covenant-love relationship but also the fruitful growth in love, joy, peace, patience, kindness, goodness, faithfulness, gentleness, and self-control—the forming of the character of Christ in them. There is no limit to such growth, no point at which we can say "We have arrived." So we pray that we and other Christians may go on discovering more and more of the breadth, length, height, and depth of the glorious love of God—a love which can overwhelm us and which we can experience in such reality that we can accurately describe it as "beyond knowledge."

The aim of Paul's prayer is that believers may be filled with the fullness of God—never content with second-rate Christian living, always wanting to grow no matter what their chronological age. One of the marks of spiritual life in elderly Christians is that, however old they are, they want to learn more of Christ and to grow in him. There is no retirement from the Christian life. As the external fabric decays, the inner nature is continuously renewed day by day.

Just before I left Manchester, a new bishop was appointed to the diocese. Following a special service in the cathedral there was a great reception held in the grandeur of the Town Hall. All the clergy were invited as well as various civic leaders. The tables were loaded with all sorts of food but, being polite Englishmen, we sipped our cups of tea and took a few of the delicately-cut cucumber sandwiches. However, there was one little old lady there—I do not know how she happened to be present—who was obviously living on a small income. She was not going to miss the opportunity of this occasion. Elbowing sundry clergy out of her way she tackled the goodies (ignoring the polite sandwiches) with gusto. At one point, faced with a fruit bowl in which large segments of pineapple lay awash in juice, she looked for a spoon, but, not seeing one, plunged her hand into the bowl to get the pineapple out as we continued to nibble politely on cucumber sandwiches.

Are we like that about spiritual things—content with polite forms of respectable Christianity and almost despising those who seem to be "too enthusiastic" for our liking? Or are we eager for God to spread before us "the riches of his glory," hungry for more of our Lord's provision, thrusting our hand into the bowl and growing in his fullness? No need here for spiritual slimming; growth is the aim!

We need to echo the thrust of this prayer in Ephesians 3 for ourselves and for our fellow-Christians—for our pastors, leaders, and all who serve, for new Christians, for older Christians who may be demonstrating a spiritual "middle-age-spread" of slowing down, for elderly believers that their lives may be a rich testimony to the fruits of continued spiritual growth.

In the New Testament we also learn the vital necessity of praying for spiritual protection for fellow-Christians. Jesus gave us an example of this when, in Luke 22:32, he prayed for Peter. Satan, he informed Peter, was going to "sift" him. Note that Jesus did not pray that the attack would not occur, but that Peter's faith would not fail and that afterwards, because he had resisted the attack himself, he would be able to strengthen his brethren. Those of us who are parents or youth leaders may wish that our teenagers could be protected from the pressures inherent in growing up, the temptation to be independent, to swing away from Christ, and to conform to the world. Yet they *need* to face that stage of life. We should not pray for them to avoid it, but for them to come through it with their faith, not only intact, but stronger and deeper. We can apply the same prayer policy to fellow-Christians facing problems, such as disappointment, illness, or bereavement. Although we need to pray for their physical need, we will have a primary prayer-aim of seeing them come through with deepened faith and the ability to help others facing similar situations in the future. The physical is only temporary. It is the spiritual nature which is eternal. So spiritual growth is our prime target in prayer.

Praying for mental well-being

In ordinary life we know the limitations of understanding and of coping with life that come when a young person cannot be bothered to work or learn at school, even as a "one-talent" person. Later in life so many people would like to kick themselves for losing out on the opportunities they had available to them. By contrast, we can see how those who do apply themselves in work and study, according to their abilities, grow in confidence in facing up to all of life. Applying the principles of understanding and learning will open up a variety of avenues and life will continue to be enriched.

It is similar in the Christian life. By faith in Christ we are brought into fellowship with God, the fountain of all wisdom and truth. The Holy Spirit indwells us as the interpreter of this divine wisdom, and there is no growth-limit in understanding the things of God, whatever our abilities. Naturally, the ten-talent intellect is expected to take giant steps in spiritual understanding and the one-talent may progress more slowly, covering less ground. But growth is expected in both.

Yet so often, like some school-children, Christians "cannot be bothered." Because of apathy or laziness they pay little attention to sermons, to teaching in groups, and to Christian books. Their bookcases reflect their lack of desire to grow in understanding—often it holds only the more "sensational" and superficial Christian paperbacks. They lack confidence in the Christian life because of basic ignorance and because what they believe has neither been tested nor thought through in any depth. We must emphasize that any Christian who wants to grow in understanding can do so if he has access to books and is prepared to listen and think. Even those whose intellectual ability is quite small can make significant growth; it is not limited to the highly intelligent though they are rightly expected to go further with their intellectual equipment. Some of the people I have seen come to Christ have been functionally illiterate, but their urge to grow has pushed them into learning to read and write, and then go on reading. Others who have never read a book in their life have found the Holy Spirit helping them to read and understand, because they were willing to grow. Growth involves desire, discipline, and determination on our part. The Holy Spirit responds to that by opening up our understanding. It is he who leads us into truth. In all who grow like this there comes an increasing confidence in the Christian life, a heightened ability to communicate the faith to others, and a deepening richness in understanding the things of God.

Paul was sufficiently concerned about such growth to make it a matter or prayer for the saints. In Philippians 1:9, for instance, he prayed that "your love may abound more and more, with knowledge and all discernment, so that you may approve what is excellent . . . and may be pure and blameless . . . filled with the fruits of righteousness."

Too often we see Christian intelligence downgraded, almost despised. People who say, "Your faith is too cerebral" may be rightly rejecting a coldly intellectual approach, but often they are simply anti-intellectual. The pendulum seems to swing toward *experience* and away from *understanding*. But the New Testament is much more balanced! As Paul reminds us, love is to abound more and more, *but with knowledge and all discernment*. As John Stott has put it,

"Your mind matters." Experience and understanding go warmly hand in hand. We need both. The spiritual gifts to the Church, in Ephesians 4, are to bring us "to the unity of the faith and of the knowledge of the Son of God, to mature manhood, to the measure of the stature of the fullness of Christ." Why? So that we may not be like children, "tossed to and fro and carried about by every wind of doctrine." But this stability will not be cold, or detached, for Paul continues: "Rather, speaking the truth in love . . . ."

We are all under pressure to "conform to the world." The media powerfully influence us. Spiritual transformation is "by the renewal of your mind" (Romans 12:2). The young Christian is in the thick of the continuing battle for the mind. He particularly needs prayer, but so do all of us. At one extreme are those who seem to "give up without a fight" and go under. At the other extreme are those who allow an authoritarian group to do their thinking for them. We need to find the balance, responsibly using our God-given intellects under the Lordship of Christ, whose Spirit is leading us into truth and experience beyond the merely intellectual. May we always want to grow in our Christian understanding—reading, thinking, taking notes, learning. We must pray it for ourselves. But we must also pray it for our Christian friends, that the Church's teachers and preachers may not stop learning, fossilizing in middle-age, but may maintain a healthy alertness to new issues, an attitude of curiosity and wonder, discernment and understanding. We must pray for young people that they may not just grow in understanding in their academic subjects but may use their minds to grow into Christian adulthood. We must pray that those without much intellectual capacity may not be discouraged and give up. We must pray that day by day, or in mid-week Bible study groups, when our friends open the Scriptures they may see new things as the Holy Spirit illuminates them. We must pray that for Sunday's sermons the preacher may find his understanding wonderfully opened up in preparation and the congregation responding to the preaching itself with stimulated minds, warm hearts, and responsive action. We must pray that Christians in the "front line" of battle may have wisdom to know how to speak out for Christ and uphold his truth. We must pray that Christians involved in broadcasting, television, writing, and the arts may grow in understanding as they seek to communicate to a starved and sterile world. The range of such prayer is almost infinite. So let us pray, that in terms of 1 Corinthians 14:20 the saints may "not be children" in their thinking, but "in thinking be mature."

Praying for physical well-being

We pray readily for physical well-being in our lives and in the lives of fellow-Christians, because pain, suffering, danger, hunger, tension, and illness are always present to affect our bodies, and our bodies react! So we can empathize with other people in their suffering and we long to help them. Prayer is one effective means of doing so.

Our hearts will be lifted up in prayer for Christians suffering persecution, deprivation, and imprisonment. Our physical help for them is often limited. Our spiritual help is unlimited. Prayer is not stopped by the bars of a prison cell. There are many Christians in refugee camps and in areas of the world where food supplies are desperately inadequate. Here our physical help in terms of money and supplies is more possible, but the roots of the problem go much deeper and can only be touched through prayer. We will want to pray for those relief agencies who are trying to deal with the problems on the spot.

It is natural also to pray for one another in all the journeyings of life, whether to the local shopping center or across the world by plane. How often we can see the Lord's hand in such events, yet how much more will we see this when we look back on our lives from the heavenly perspective and see what delays or accidents God has prevented, without our knowing anything about it!

But it is the question of *healing* that is the major concern to most Christians when thinking about prayer for physical well-being. The key to all prayer for healing lies in our desire for the glory of God. If we accept the foundations of prayer discussed in the first section of this book, then the glory of God will be our greatest concern and we will submit all prayer for healing to that higher purpose. Hallesby, in his classic book on prayer, mentions Samuel Zeller, who lived years ago in Switzerland. Zeller was a great speaker, pastor, and pray-er. Through him many were healed. Yet Zeller never prayed just for healing but for God to be glorified. He would add to any healing prayer: "If it will glorify thy Name more, then let them remain sick, but, if that be thy will, give them power to glorify thy Name through their illness." That was courageous but accurate praying and in no way minimized or lessened Zeller's effectiveness as an instrument of healing. Many were healed; but many were not healed. His prayer for the Lord's glory was from the heart. Perhaps it was for that same glory that he himself suffered from a life-long ailment.

There has been immense damage dealt to people, to Christian integrity, and to the Lord's honor by those who teach that *all* illnesses can and should be healed, and that because illness is a mark of the fallen sinful world, God can be glorified only in healing, never in allowing sickness to remain. Proponents of such a viewpoint often cite Matthew 8:17 and its reference to Isaiah 53 to claim that, on the cross, Christ carried our sicknessess as well as our sins. Logic demands that if physical wholeness is thus guaranteed for the believer, so is spiritual perfection. But it is biblical to assert that although we have the power of Christ, we still have mortal bodies and fallen natures until we die. Triumphs and victories can certainly be expected by the believer, but perfect wholeness must wait for heaven.

The results of the "all can be healed" teaching leads some

people to despair, because they are *not* healed and they assume it is due to sin in their lives, or a lack of faith. It may lead others into deception, claiming they are healed even though they are quite clearly in the same physical state as before. A godly doctor friend related this story to me: "A dear Christian woman developed multiple sclerosis of rapid and severe character. She told me that the Lord was going to heal her and she had profound faith. In process of time she was getting steadily worse and one day said that she considered my lack of faith the obstacle. It happened that a healer was visiting the town. I arranged ambulance and wheel chair for my patient to be present at the healing service. Hands were laid upon her and she claimed to be "cured." Sadly, in fact, the disease progressed to a fatal termination, though she never again blamed me for obstructing her "cure."

The deception is sometimes recorded in books, and the reader does not usually have the opportunity to check the facts. The same healer mentioned above compiled a book of case histories of healing, among which was a case which we would call a "thalidomide case" today. The healing claimed was the replacement of a primitive "flipper" by a new hand. A London surgeon writing a book on healing a few years later revealed that the healer had been sued by the parents of the child affected, who had *not* been healed. However, the surgeon qualified his condemnation of the healer by saying that the healer had seen the fingers grow "in her mind's eye" and her faith was so intense that she believed that it had really happened.

The faith of others may be destroyed when they have believed that all illnesses can and should be cured by prayer, and yet it does not happen. We recently received a letter from a house church in south London asking for any cassette tapes on the subject of healing. A member of their group had contracted leukemia. Though they had prayed with fervency and faith, the person died. The letter ended with the sad words: "We have all lost our faith."

Such loss of faith is a tragedy, for a balanced biblical view leads to no such problems. To believe in the power of prayer for healing (and I do fervently) while submitting the problem and the process to the glory of God, leaves us in trust and peace. This is why the whole first section of this book establishes the foundations of prayer. Chapter one is particularly relevant to this discussion on healing.

Paul balances it beautifully in 2 Corinthians 12. The earlier sections of his letter told how much suffering he himself had known. So we know he wrote from first-hand experience. In verse 8 he tells us that he pleaded with God three times to take away the "thorn in my flesh, a messenger of Satan." The Lord's reply was "My grace is sufficient for you, for my power is made perfect in weakness," at which point Paul accepts the reply, not grudgingly, but gladly. If this is the means by which Christ's power is to be demonstrated in him, then he will even *boast* about his weaknesses. For Christ's sake he will *delight* in weaknesses, insults, hardships, persecutions, and difficulties. Thus his prayer for healing or deliverance is submitted to the higher purposes of God. The result? No tension, no deception, no destruction of faith, only power and praise. And if it had been God's will to glorify himself through healing Paul, the result would also have been power and praise!

As E. Stanley Jones wrote in *Christ and Human Suffering:* "He told us not to escape suffering but to use it. Christ suggests that we are to take up pain, calamity, injustice, and persecution into the purpose of our lives and make them contribute to higher ends, the ends for which we really live. He does not explain suffering or explain it away, but He changed everything. He would turn the world's supreme tragedy into the world's supreme testimony—and did!"

How then should we approach the matter of illness? Should we veer away from healing prayer or come at it half-heartedly? Certainly not! The following steps may guide us:

1 We must take hold of faith in the living God and his ability (Ephesians 3:20) to do more than we ask or think. Yes, we believe God is *able* to heal any illness.

2 We must pray—specifically. We will do so, if possible, with other Christians in the context of the church's prayer gathering, or at a service, or in a fellowship group, or at a special gathering of fellow Christians for this purpose. We may lay hands on the afflicted person as we pray, thus identifying ourselves with him, though this is not essential. At a special gathering we may be able to spend a full evening in prayer. We will want to involve any members of the church who seem to be specially gifted with healing love and those members who are particularly close to the sick person. If that person is too ill to come to the church then representatives of the church should go to his bedside, as described in James 5:14.

Prayer needs to be informed and intelligent so there must be openness about the nature of the illness. That openness must include the sick person, because if relatives are concealing the truth from him or her they cannot be open with the church and prayer cannot be specific.

3 We must realize, as James 5:16 in its context shows, that confession and forgiveness of sin may be needed. Harbored grudges, bitterness, or lack of forgiveness may in itself create illness and healing may come only when the cause is identified.

4 We must submit our prayers to the purposes of God's glory, praying to that end as Samuel Zeller did.

5 We must stay sensitive to the Lord as we pray, perhaps for weeks or months. Is there a point when God says that there will not be healing (as there was for Paul after his "three times" of pleading)? If so, we will turn our prayer and action even more to supporting the sick per-

son in glorifying the Lord. How powerfully that can be true in terminal illness! Or our sensitivity to the Lord may guide us to continue to pray for healing.

6   We must be open to the Lord's ways of doing things. His healing may be entirely through established medical means, or it may be swift and decisive and we will call it a miracle (realizing that some illnesses are subject to sudden remission or regression). It may be delayed because the Lord wants to bring deep spiritual growth in the time of weakness before restoring the person (as Hudson Taylor and George Müller both experienced).

7   We must give praise and thanksgiving when we recognize that the Lord has answered for his glory.

8   We must be sensitive in love to those involved in illness or bereavement where there has been faith and prayer without healing, even though another with a similar illness has been healed.

9   We must learn not to generalize from the occasional "miracle" cure to give the impression that everyone can similarly be healed. It has been my joy and privilege to see a number of people suddenly restored to health, through prayer. God has at times healed exactly at the time the church was praying. The joy has been enormous. I am deeply thankful for these experiences as well as for those where people have been healed and restored more gradually, but I have learned that I must not generalize. I know God can and does heal, and on that basis I pray fervently and with faith. I know I also must pray for his glory to be revealed, either in healing or in triumph within the framework of the illness, so I submit my prayer to that higher end, again with faith. To God be the glory!

CHAPTER 15

PRAYING FOR THE LORD'S SERVANTS

ALL OF GOD'S SERVANTS MUST BE SAINTS, but not all saints are servants. We become saints by God's grace; we become servants by volunteering and surrendering our lives to the lordship of Christ. Paul was such a servant and asked for prayer support for his assignment both in Ephesians 6:18-20 and elsewhere. We have a particular responsibility, as Christians, to pray for those who are involved in the service of Christ, especially in the front line of battle.

This will mean special prayer support for Christian leaders, pastors, speakers, evangelists, and missionaries, but also for one another in our ambassadorship for Christ, whether in office, factory, college, school, hospital, shop trade union, local or national government, or in our neighborhood. Service for Christ has openings for all saints and the Lord needs us all.

This is a large responsibility. How can we begin to cover it in our prayers? Let me suggest five possibilities:

Pray for boldness to speak
In Ephesians 6:19 Paul asks his friends to "Pray also for me, that whenever I open my mouth, words may be given me so that I will fearlessly make known the mystery of the gospel, for which I am an ambassador in chains. Pray that I may declare it fearlessly, as I should" (NIV). It was not easy for Paul to witness—Paul—the most ardent, passionate, intense of the apostles. That's encouraging, isn't it? He tells the Corinthians how he trembled when he came to them with the gospel. Paul so often seems a giant in the work of the gospel but his strength was derived not from physical stature but from spiritual renewal. He was obviously thrown back on the Lord constantly, just as Peter and the others were (Acts 4:31). Now get hold of this! Grasp it! We so readily excuse our weaknesses in witnessing by assuming it is easier for someone else with a more outgoing personality and more approachable contacts. But it is *never* easy to witness and if it ever becomes easy we should stop, because we'll know that we are using *our* strength and capabilities, not the Lord's.

What about prayer for ourselves as servants? When opportunity comes for witness we should pray that we may be given courage to speak, not hesitantly or with shame, but powerfully and with joy. It is good to commit each day to God, asking for *his* opportunities. Forcing openings for the gospel is seldom effective, so learn to pray "Lord, if you provide the opportunity to speak for you today, I promise I will take it and I pray you will give me boldness and clarity." Then *keep* the promise. If someone at lunch spouts off about "what is the world coming to?" or "The standards of this country are collapsing. Why?" or "How can there be a God?" or any other of the thousands of possible openings, take a deep breath, send up an arrow prayer, open your mouth, and speak!

We should pray that our close Christian friends will have this boldness. We should also pray for courage for those engaged in evangelism projects or missions, for confidence for those in evangelistic preaching, for loving concern for those in particular situations of witness such as Paul had in prison, for a clear witness on the part of those Christians in positions of public prominence—in politics and national or international leadership. I find I really experience the Lord's strength when people pray specially for a broadcast sermon or an evangelistic one. There is no less work in one's preparation, but one feels carried along by the Spirit both in preparation and in speaking.

Pray for an "open door" for the Word

In Colossians 4:2-4 Paul asks his readers to "Pray for us, too, that God may open a door for our messasge."

It is one thing to sow the seed; it is another to know there is ground ready to receive it, where the seed will not be choked or trodden down, but can take root and flourish.

In evangelistic services, we will need to pray as much for the hearers, as for the preacher. Spiritual insensitivity or a seared conscience block the Word of God, no matter how clearly preached. There often needs to be some "dynamiting," to break down the stone walls or hard hearts so that the message can get through. None of us can open minds and hearts that are spiritually blind or closed. Only God can. We should pray before such a service and during it, praying if possible, for specific people. Evangelism is the spearhead of the attack on the power of Satan, so we know that the battle will be fierce.

Similarly we will need to pray for this "opening of doors for the Word" when we go out witnessing on the street, or door-to-door. When I served in Holy Trinity, Platt, in Manchester, we organized the parish into four quadrants. In whichever quadrant you lived, that area was your particular spiritual responsibility. If you lived outside the parish, you were assigned to one of the quadrants. There were leaders for each quadrant, with autonomy of strategy, but every quadrant team met regularly to pray for the streets in their area by name, for people living in those streets by name, for store owners and for business establishments by name; all contacts, visiting, and house meetings were undergirded with prayer for "open doors" in people's hearts.

Much of this kind of prayer is needed for the particularly difficult areas for the gospel—the inner city areas or those parts of the world where nationalistic religions enslave people's minds. You may feel your place of work or the area where you live is hard too, because of materialistic self-satisfaction. We can pray that God will open doors for the gospel and that you and others may share it freely.

Pray for God's Word to triumph

Paul pleaded, in 2 Thessalonians 3:1: "Pray for us, that the word of the Lord may speed on and triumph." This had happened among the Thessalonians; they knew what Paul was talking about—that joyful breakthrough which brings not a trickle but a flood of people turning to the Lord. And of course, this is what we all long to see. Yet often we get depressed as we read of apparent "success" stories in other churches or in Christian work elsewhere in the world, and feel we are getting nowhere. It is easy to lose the expectancy of faith and grow cold in the expectancy of prayer.

Yet what is the measure of success and failure? Take a situation where the work is numerically small in a tough, depressed area of the inner city. To see a handful of people come through to faith in such circumstances is a triumph. We should not be obsessed with numbers. Your church may not be like X or Y, but does that matter? God has called you *there*. He has called you to serve him and to trust him. Pray, and ask others to pray, that "the impossible" may become the possible, that the Word of God may speed on and triumph, that people in the district may begin to recognize that lives are being changed and that God's Good News *is* the only answer to man's need.

There is a particular thrill about it when the speeding-on and triumph comes with large numbers, but there are also the considerable responsibilities of care and training for converts, as has been discovered in the work of the dramatic advance of the gospel in South America in recent years.

So let us pray for the area where we live, for our town, for our country, for our world, everywhere we want to see the Word speed on and triumph. And we want those outside the faith to see it too, so that they do not relegate Christianity to the garbage can as inconsequential, but see it as powerfully relevant to today's man in today's world—relevant to *them*!

Pray for the Lord's servants to be protected
In 2 Thessalonians 3:2-3, Paul prays, "that we may be delivered from wicked and evil men; for not all have faith." Paul knew plenty about opposition to the gospel, with plots against his life, mob violence, threats, and all sorts of dangers. His request for "protection prayer" arose from vivid experience. Since he wrote those words, the list of Christian martyrs has been lengthened by hundreds of thousands, right up to our present day. The pioneer missionary is uniquely exposed to the danger of attack. We bow in salute to the courage and zeal that has led thousands to go with the gospel to cannibal tribes, to dense jungle areas where people live in animistic fear, to areas of danger and disease and heat exhaustion.

Our prayer for protection must recognize that our martyrdom may result in God's glory (and Paul saw that himself in his letters to the Philippians, eager that Christ should be honored, whether by his martyrdom or his deliverance). But as with healing, we pray for protection and then entrust the servants of the gospel to the Lord's care. Many are the stories of remarkable deliverance, of people being stirred to pray—even being woken from sleep to do so—at the very moment that a missionary was facing death, and of the attacker being stopped and even "seeing angels standing around the missionary."

In 1979 there was the amazing deliverance of Bishop Deqhani-Tafti in Iran, when his attackers fired at him in bed at point-blank range, and the shots ringed the pillow but did not hit him. This, he said, was because so many were praying for his protection. Nevertheless, there are many who have been equally prayed for who, in God's purposes, have been entered in the list of martyrs. The bishop's own son was tragically murdered in Iran in May, 1980.

We need also to pray for our fellow-Christians at spiritually critical moments of their lives. One such "moment" is when a young Christian leaves home to go to university or college. Suddenly all restraints are lifted. Around him are fellow-students with utterly secular and humanistic ideas on life and morality. It is a moment of self-awareness, self-determination, and decision. Young Christians may be destroyed during the first months, or they may mature, making the faith and its practice "their own" in a new and vital way. The church at home needs to pray specifically and constantly for its young people in those first vital months of college life, or of leaving home for any reason.

Pray for more volunteers for God

Jesus looked out on the crowds, in Matthew 9:36-38, and said: "The harvest is plentiful, but the laborers are few; pray therefore the Lord of the harvest to send out laborers into his harvest." Here's a command to obey. The Church of God across the world always needs more who will truly serve. There are many who are willing to help when it suits them, or serve as it fits in with their other interests, but not too many have pledged themselves as servants of Christ, for whom Christ is first in their lives, who fit their own interests around Christ and service for his kingdom. Pray for more Christians to have such commitment.

Then we must pray for the Lord to call men and women out of their "secular" occupation, to leave their modern-day fishing nets: their computer-programming, their executive position in commerce, their professional opportunities, and to be set apart as ordained ministers, teachers, or missionaries, or volunteers in relief organizations, social services, and youth work. There is a lessening of such commitment in our day. So pray, as the Lord told us to do, that he will call more and that those who hear the call may say willingly, "Here am I; send me."

These five areas of prayer for the servants of the Lord by no means exhaust the range of such prayer. They are, at best, only guidelines. Support for one another in serving Christ is an essential part of our mutuality in the body of Christ. Let us not fail one another in interest, care, and practical help; but supremely we must not fail one another in prayer. With Samuel (1 Sam. 12:23) let us reassure our fellow-servants: "Far be it from me that I should sin against the Lord by ceasing to pray for you."

CHAPTER 16

PRAYING FOR SPECIAL PEOPLE: LEADERS, UNBELIEVERS & ENEMIES

GOD'S WORD ENJOINS US TO PRAY for three kinds of special people not mentioned earlier:

Prayer priority: for leaders throughout the world
How do we pray for the world? Primarily, by praying for its leaders and for all in authority. This is how Paul details it: "I urge that supplications, prayers, intercessions, and thanksgivings be made for all men, for kings and all who are in high positions, that we may lead a quiet and peaceable life, godly and respectful in every way. This is good, and it is acceptable in the sight of God our Savior, who desires all men to be saved and to come to the knowledge of the truth" (1 Tim. 2:1-4).

From this passage we learn that our praying should not be confined to *Christian* kings and rulers. Paul emphasizes the need to pray for *all* in authority, which would include military dictators and atheistic rulers as well as democratic governments and godly leaders. God's ability to use a heathen leader for his purposes is dramatically demonstrated in his choice of Cyrus, whom he describes in Isaiah 44:28 as "my shepherd, and he shall fulfil my purpose" and in Isaiah 45:1 as his "anointed, whose right hand I have grasped."

Prayer for leaders requires a vision as large as the globe, a sense of the sweep and meaning of history, and an attention to detail. Our world vision grows as we make it our responsibility to be informed and as we deliberately avoid parochialism in our prayer concern. A sense of history will keep us from expecting too much, too soon, at the same time making us aware of the suddenness with which events may happen on the world scene. It will also help us to perceive the long-term purposes of God. An attention to detail will keep us from being vague. Information about the countries of the world and their leaders is available, thanks to the news media, enabling us to pray by name for rulers and to have some understanding of the political structures and pressures in a given country. Similarly, as we remember those who wield enormous influence in commerce, trade unions, or politics, it is good to pray for them by name. Ask God to lay particular names on your heart for prayer.

What should be the thrust of our prayer for world leaders? Certainly not just for their well-being or success; we also pray for leaders because of their influence for good or evil. Are we then praying for justice, peace, and economic stability? This may be part of the prayer, but the emphasis of 1 Timothy 2:1-3 is that the spreading of the gospel is to be the supreme objective of our praying. God desires all to be saved and to come to the knowledge of the truth. Ideally, this takes place in a "godly and respectful" environment, and in the context of "quiet and peaceable" conditions. Of course, the gospel may flourish under persecution, the blood of martyrs often being "the seed of the Church," but an atheistic or oppressive regime may effectively block the spread of the gospel. We have seen evidence of this with the "dissuaders" around Christian churches in Russia, the closing of churches, the restriction of real Christian liberty in many other countries such as Turkey and Iran, the annihilation of Christians among the millions murdered in Cambodia, and the long suppression of Christianity during China's cultural revolution, although a day of new opportunity has begun to dawn over that ancient nation.

We will also pray for a "godly and respectful" society with an eye to the spread of the gospel. Countries involved in revolution, anarchy, deep unrest, corruption, or religious nationalism, are not easy arenas in which to preach Christ, even if such difficult circumstances persuade some people to turn to Christ. Church gatherings may be restricted, pastoral oversight rendered difficult, and publishing limited, but the most frustrating restriction is often the ban on seeking conversions (and therefore of evangelistic preaching); turning from a nationally espoused religion is likely to be viewed as disloyalty and treachery.

A "respectful" society endeavors to protect the rights of individuals to their own views without restricting their freedom to disseminate what they believe, unless their views are themselves destructive and restrictive. The "respectful" society enables dialogue to take place and permits people to listen to each other over any issue. In this atmosphere the sensitive evangelist and witness can flourish and the reasonableness of the gospel can be explained, protected from white-hot bigotry or anger. The "respectful" society is concerned about both human rights *and* responsibilities, about justice, about the poor, and about the environment, because God is concerned about these matters too. Thus the Christian is able to demonstrate his faith and convictions in the process of tackling such issues.

All these factors should encourage us to pray more consistently and thoroughly for those in authority in the world. Because we are concerned for peace and for a godly and respectful society, we will pray for leaders involved in the arms race, the build-up of nuclear power, and international relationships. The world stands all the time near the brink of holocaust. Some think the world will ultimately end up submitting to Marxist domination for the sake of peace, but that would be a long, long way from the "godly and respectful" peace described by Paul. On the human level, pessimism colors the thinking of most of us. But the Christian must meet it all with prayer. A new surge of prayer for the world's leaders is urgently needed, for the sake of peace and thus for the sake of the spread of the Good News of Christ and salvation.

Prayer priority: for unbelievers

There is a passion in Paul's prayers for his own people, his "kinsmen by race," which will challenge us in our prayers for those near and dear to us—in our families, work-place or country—who have not come to faith in Christ. There is nothing detached or apathetic about this statement "I have great sorrow and unceasing anguish in my heart. For I could wish that I myself were accursed and cut off from Christ for the sake of my brethren, my kinsmen by race" (Rom. 9:2-3), or this: "My heart's desire and prayer to God for them is that they may be saved" (Rom. 10:1).

As Christ looked at a crowd and saw them as "sheep without a shepherd," as Paul thought of his kinsmen with anguish because they were not saved, so, surely, we will look at our relatives and close friends with deep agony of heart if they are still outside of Christ. It hurts us, deeply. They may be delightful people—kind, generous, moral, and helpful—yet they have resisted or rejected Christ.

It is natural for us to pray much for their conversion and this will usually involve considerable perseverance and patience. Our very closeness to them makes the whole approach to witness more delicate, and that is why we turn to prayer, concentrating such prayer on a limited number of individuals so that we can give time. Though this may mean that we concentrate in prayer on family members and close friends, where possible, we ought also to take on our hearts other specific people, named to us perhaps, by missionaries, or by others involved in the church's outreach. This will mean that we seek out the kind of detailed information that enables our prayer to be meaningful, loving, and specific. Remember, though, this is battle prayer, and the battle is for immortal souls. Because we may often be the major instrument of prayer, then, ours is a responsible and heartagonizing task.

If we follow Paul in Romans 10, we will learn to discern what is blocking our friend's understanding and acceptance of the gospel (for example, his faulty view of the church, his shallow rejection of the Bible as a "fairy tale," "science has disproved religion") and then make that block our target in prayer and if possible, action. The blocks may align with the two Paul could see in his kinsmen:

They are ignorant of God's way, the gospel, in which case we need to pray that their ignorance might be penetrated, that they might actually "hear" and understand something of the gospel through a radio or TV program, a friend's comment, a word from someone at the office, a book, the witness of a traveller on the same plane, or some other means. It is *not* that they are usually anti-God or anti-Christ but that they are *ignorant* of the gospel, however knowledgeable they are about other things.

They are relying on their own ideas and their own way, in which case we would pray that their reliance on themselves may be shaken, that a chink may be made in their self-defensive armor, and that they may begin to see the uselessness and emptiness of human effort.

Though we must always be prepared we should never try

to force God's pace or do his work. The Father did not pursue the Prodigal Son, but as soon as the son turned, he ran to meet him. If we discern a turning we must run to welcome but with sensitivity. The prodigal returned to his father and his house, but for our relatives or friends the Christian life may be new and unfamiliar, and if they are older they may find it embarrassing to turn to Christ after so long. Our sensitivity in love, care, and fellowship will be vital. Aggressiveness could be fatal. At such a moment we will need to pray for ourselves as much as for the new believer!

The encouragement Paul laid hold of to go on praying for relatives, friends and others outside the kingdom (Rom. 10:13) is "Every one who calls upon the name of the Lord will be saved."

Prayer priority: for enemies

These lines occur in the hymn "What a friend we have in Jesus":

> *Do thy friends despise, forsake thee?*
> *Take it to the Lord in prayer.*
> *In His arms he'll take and shield thee*
> *Thou wilt find a solace there.*

Does this sound a bit too cozy, an expression of "Christianity for our own comfort"? Certainly, retreat and comfort may be a part of the Christian experience, but so may attack and discomfort! Jesus did not tell us to "take it to the Lord in prayer" but to take *them* to the Lord in prayer. That is attack rather than retreat!

The mandate to pray for our enemies comes from our Lord Jesus in Matthew 5:44: "Love your enemies and pray for those who persecute you"—really a revolutionary pattern for living! Though I may want revenge or justice, and I may feel like striking out, I am to love and instead, pray not for myself, but for the enemy who is persecuting me. That means praying for members of my family or friends who despise my faith and make cutting remarks. It means praying for the colleague at work who always needles me for being "religious"; for the lecturer or professor who makes derogatory remarks about "naive Bible thumpers"; for the active anti-Christian groups in our area; for oppressors in atheistic countries; for persecutors in the prison-camps of a pagan dictatorship.

Why should we pray for them? "So that you may be sons of your Father who is in heaven" says Jesus, "for he makes his sun rise on the evil and on the good, and sends rain on the just and on the unjust." Are we able to share the same measure of our love with enemies as with friends? Can we rejoice in the success of our enemies rather than wishing they meet with disaster? None of us finds this easy, but it becomes easier when we pray for them.

Soon after Bishop Festo Kivengere escaped from Uganda under the Idi Amin dictatorship, he attended a three-hour service at our church, All Souls. During a message on Christ's words, "Father, forgive them; for they know not what they do," "a great searchlight" shone in his heart. He felt that the Lord was moving him to forgive Amin. Festo responded, "Lord, I don't hate this man" but he felt the Lord telling him that he had been growing hard and resentful towards Amin and that Amin was not the loser, but Festo. It was a shock for this godly leader. Then, the Lord told him: "You think it's hard to forgive him? Suppose on that day when the soldiers were putting the nails into my hands, one of them had been President Amin with a hammer and nail. Would I have said: 'Father, forgive them, all except Amin'?"

"That was enough," wrote Festo. "It was all I needed. I bowed my head and said, 'Please, Father, forgive me, forgive me! Then give me grace to forgive President Amin.' He did. That's why the little book *I Love Idi Amin* could be written."

How many enemies or aggressors are on our prayer lists? When did we last love and pray for those who laugh at our faith? When have we needed to pray, and been able to do so: "Father, lay not this sin to their charge"? Only hearts flooded with the love of God can pray like this.

I know how much I fail in such praying. Perhaps you feel like that too. If so, let us pray for ourselves that we may follow the example of our Lord Jesus, of Stephen, of Festo Kivengere, and have grace to forgive, to love, and to pray for our enemies and our persecutors.

CHAPTER 17

PRAYING FOR THE WORLDWIDE CHURCH

BECAUSE CHRIST IS ITS HEAD, the Christian church is glorious, and holy, and strong, and growing, and useful. It is also flawed, and inadequate, and weak, and fragmented, and divided because it is made up of sinful people, and that includes us.

Nor can we opt out. We have been baptized by the one Spirit into the one body. *We are involved* and cannot be mere spectators. We all long for the church (the body of believers around the world) to be more glorifying to God and more effective as God's agency to the world. We will work to forward these aims, but we must also pray.

In his great "high-priestly" prayer of John 17, a prayer of unfathomable depth and multiple richness, our Lord Jesus showed us how to pray for the church. There are at least five major themes that we can extract from it as prayer-targets, in praying for the church:

God's people are set apart

"Yours they were, and you gave them to me" (John 17:6).

"I am praying for them; I am not praying for the world but for those you have given me, for they are yours" (John 17:9).

"All mine are yours, and yours are mine, and I am glorified in them" (John 17:10).

"They are not of the world, even as I am not of the world" (John 17:14).

Often the impression is given that the church is "set apart" by ecclesiastical ceremonies, archaic King James language, a cloistered clergy, and a program of almost total irrelevance to modern living. Such impressions are often unfair, although we have to admit that in some cases they are all too accurate. If there is evidence that the church is the "people of God"—a group of men and women united in their love for God the Father, saved through the blood of Christ and renewed by the Holy Spirit—the Lord will be glorified, as long as the faith is not held onto smugly and exclusively but shared openly and warmly. The people of God in any area should be known as those who care, whose love reaches out to others in need, to the young and the elderly. The church's "set-apartness" is not negative but positive, as it becomes the hands and feet of Christ in service as well as the body of Christ in worship.

Our burden should be to pray that the churches we know may be demonstrating this God-empowered mark of being his people. It will be seen in the sense of stepping forward. We are the people of *God*, not just a human organization finding itself squeezed by the world into dwindling numbers and ineffective impact. Christ is the head of the church, leading it and empowering it. We are to look to him for his strategy, his way forward, his leading, so that he can bless us as we follow him and glorify himself through us, as those who belong to him.

Times of retreat together for the local church or its

leaders—when there is a willingness to be honest with God and a desire to be shown how to change direction, initiate new action, or correct a wrong emphasis—will keep the church in his will. In All Souls we have developed these with our staff, our church council, and other groups. The results have been clearly visible, as the church's course is corrected to conform to what we sense the Lord is saying to us.

We will want to pray that the worship services of churches around the world will have the reality of the people of God met together with him, so that outsiders coming in may sense that we "mean business" with God and that he is meeting with us and pouring out his blessing. Man-centered, cold, formal, and boring services instantly give the opposite impression.

God's people are secure

"The world has hated them, because they are not of the world. . . . I do not pray that you should take them out of the world, but that you should keep them from the evil one" (John 17:14-15).

If the church is truly "the people of God" in the world, it will always be under attack. It is not to retreat into the comfortable security of "holy huddles," not to be "out of the world," but *in it* as salt and light. That is why Jesus teaches us to pray for security from the Evil One in the battle. The attacks that come are direct and indirect, with force and with subtlety, from within as well as from without.

The more direct attacks may come through political and military force. We must pray for the church under persecution, and in those countries where God's people have been obliterated or forced underground we must pray that the flame of the church will be kept burning, ready to be fanned back into life and witness when a new day dawns. We need to pray for the sustaining life of the Spirit for all Christians in prison for their faith, or in countries where the anti-God forces seem rampant, that God's people may be kept secure in Christ.

The Evil One also attacks as an "angel of light" (2 Cor. 11:14), from within the church, in the form of false apostles and deceitful workmen. Paul was deeply concerned at the way such people undermined his apostolic teaching, diverting people from the true faith with their offers of special spirituality or a less-demanding Christianity. We are perplexed and pained to find that people who hold high office in the Christian church, or in university faculties of theology, can stab the church in the back with false teaching, denying even such foundational doctrines as the Incarnation and the Atonement.

Attacks from outside the church have come from false cults and heresies since the beginning. In the present day these proliferate with colossal financial backing and seem to have an alarming appeal for rootless or disillusioned people. The streets of the big cities are their hunting ground, but they also infiltrate the churches. To see young Christians "captured" by these cults is a sickening experience. To try and rescue those so captured is a heart-agonizing task.

Young Christians are prone to attack before they have become firmly established in the faith. The glitter of the world's counter-offers of "satisfaction," the pressure from the larger crowd of non-believers to conform to the world, the compromising Christian who advises them to abandon their "narrowness" and "adopt a more adult approach" to Christianity, and the inward desire to be accepted—all this renders them highly vulnerable. They are not to retreat from involvement. Prayer is the key to their security and survival, so let us learn to pray, with Jesus, that the people of God may "be kept from the Evil One."

God's people are sanctified
"Sanctify them in the truth; your word is truth" (John 17:17).

"I have given them your word" (John 17:14).

"[I pray] also for those who believe in me through their word" (John 17:20).

In the Old Testament the high priest was sanctified externally, by washing, new clothes, and an anointing with oil. In the New Testament, which teaches the "priesthood of all believers," sanctification is internal, the result of the truth of God's Word. In John 15:3 Jesus had said to the disciples, "You are already made clean by the word which I have spoken to you," and he went on to say "If you keep my commandments, you will abide in my love" (John 15:10).

There was deep concern in the early church to "guard the deposit" of truth, to deliver what had been received, to remain loyal, not diverging from the apostles' doctrine. The test of what was to be included in the New Testament canon was apostolic authorship or attestation. The New Testament is thus, in a sense, the successor to the apostles and the succession of this apostolic truth is of vital importance to the church. Where the church has strayed from the foundation of the Scriptures it has always gone into error and strayed off course. Where it has endeavored to stand on the Scriptures and to continue to study them with openness it has grown in truth and been more stable and authoritative.

Our prayer for the church must therefore be a heart-longing for the spread of the Word of God and the increasing understanding of it by all God's people. We will pray for those involved in the translation of the Scriptures, for those who distribute the Bible in forms that make it more readable, and for those trying to get more Bibles into countries where the availability of Bibles is limited. It seems incredible to me that many churches, even those who say they "stand upon the Scriptures and preach the Word," do not have Bibles at every seat, so that stranger and church member alike can open the Bible together with ease (page numbers being given) and read the passage being preached on their own eyes. The response that "people should bring their own" totally ignores strangers and their unfamiliarity with the Bible. It is music to any preacher's ear to hear the rustle of turning Bible pages all over the church, because he can then expound and point to the actual text. So I pray for churches to put first things first and to get Bibles for everyone. Better to sit on the floor with Bibles than in pews without them!

We must pray then, for the teachers of the Word. It is an awe-inspiring responsibility to preach and teach. That there is often such poor preaching and scanty exposition in the church is appalling. I constantly meet hungry Christians who are sick at heart that they are being spiritually starved in their local church and who long for preaching that opens up the Word of God with both depth of perception and relevant application. Pray for such preaching and teaching in the church everywhere and for those who have this responsibility locally. Pray for the leaders of the church across the world that they may stand on the Word and teach it. Pray too for those who teach the preachers in theological colleges. Pray for a deep submission to the Word rather than to human tradition.

All this, however, is ineffectual unless the Word is heard, received, and obeyed in our lives. The key to spiritual health is our desire to grow. I am amazed that so often in a Christian student gathering where I have been asked to expound a passage of Scripture at length, most have brought neither Bibles nor notebooks. Do they really want to grow? I doubt it. The hearers and learners who want to be sanctified in the truth will take the Word of God seriously— through preaching, teaching, group studies, and in personal discipline. The majority of spiritual ailments can be traced back to carelessness about the Scriptures. If God's Word had not been so important, Christ would not have prayed, "Sanctify them in your truth." What is important to

him must be important to us. So let us pray anew for ourselves and our fellow-Christians, that we may be both
hearers and doers of the Word.

God's people have been sent

"As you sent me into the world, so I have sent them into the
world. And for their sake I consecrate myself. . . . I do not
pray for these only, but also for those who believe in me
through their word" (John 17:18-20).

The disciples were to take over the mission of Jesus, and
his heart was deeply in prayer for them. And now we
inherit this task and its responsibility. Unless the church
has an air of being "sent" it will become merely inward-
looking and die. It must have its set-apartness, in its
worship, fellowship, and teaching. But this must be balanced by sent-ness, in involvement, mission and challenge.

One of the guidelines we can follow comes from the
phrase "As you sent me . . . so I have sent them." Jesus became incarnate, bodily present with us. He was involved
with us, sharing our life and its experiences, meeting with
agnostics, atheists, hypocrites and enemies as well as with
inquirers, believers and disciples. He was a good "mixer,"
taking time with people, even one-to-one. He could share
poverty or sit at a rich man's table with equal ease. He was
not confined to any one form or method of evangelism. He
adapted his approach to his circumstances. He was strategic
in action and timing and in all this he was constantly aware
of his "sent-ness." "My food is to do the will of him who
sent me, and to accomplish his work" (John 4:34).

"Sent-ness" for us is thus not confined to missions or
evangelistic efforts (although it includes those), but widens
out to embrace the whole purpose of our life. We are sent
into the world—in the insurance office, the sports club, the
assembly line, the street. All we do is as God's people, and
wherever we go and whatever we do, it is as those who are
sent by the Lord. There should be no separation between

our business life and our Christian life; no place for living a double life. Our membership in the body of Christ is to pervade our whole life. This is something to pray about as our minds range across all the members of our local church, and around the church in the world. Let us thank God for Christians who are unashamed to be known as Christians, and pray for those who keep it hidden. Let us pray that Christian lives may influence by their caring, their integrity, and their joy, showing the reality of Christian living in the rough-and-tumble of everyday life.

Sent-ness also has a specific mission thrust. Jesus became incarnate, but within that Incarnation lay the purpose of his teaching ministry and supremely his sacrifice for the sins of the world. He came to offer eternal life to all who would believe on him. The church has the responsibility of proclaiming, spreading, and arguing that message: life instead of death, salvation instead of damnation, made possible through Christ's death and resurrection. It is not an intrusion into people's privacy to evangelize, when we see it as a matter of life and death. The gospel is not one option among many but the single gateway to eternal life. It may be more comfortable and less demanding to ignore mission. We may argue that we should respect other faiths or that it is better to witness by life, not by lip. Nevertheless, the task of mission has been committed to the church. We may not all agree on methods, but if we do not agree that mission is part of the church's responsibility, we disobey the Lord of the church. Let us pray for churches to have a deeper sense of this responsibility. Where they are already involved, let us pray that they may learn more about how to reach out for Christ in their particular area; where they have lost any idea of mission, let us pray that they may be shaken by the Spirit, out of their inward-looking complacency, into costly action.

World mission is a further part of "sent-ness" prayer. Prayer support for what is already taking place is vital.

Whether the mission involves medicine for sick bodies or food for starving people, its center will always be the greatest need of every man, the need for spiritual regeneration. Because it is often the front-line of the battle, prayer needs to be informed and constant. Let us pray also for the continuing concern for world mission by God's church, that people and finance will be more adequate for the colossal task which Jesus himself initiated.

God's people are seen as one

"That they may be one, even as we are one . . . . [I pray] also for those who believe in me through their word, that they may all be one; even as you, Father, are in me, and I in you, that they also may be in us, so that the world may believe you have sent me . . . that they may become perfectly one" (John 17:11, 20-21, 23).

Prayer for the unity of the church was Jesus' deep heart-cry. As head of the church, how much it must be on his heart today. As it is in the Trinity (John 17:20-21), unity is not so much uniformity as unity in diversity. One huge denomination of all Christians is therefore not necessary. Agreement across the denominations, agreement in the truth of God's Word and in godly love, that shares freely at the Lord's Table, that cooperates in local concerns, that does not compete on the mission field, *is* possible and must be a deep concern of our hearts in prayer. We should pray for unity in the essentials (for it must never be at the expense of truth) and for an openness that accepts a diversity of nonessentials. We will also need to pray for the ability to see which is which!

Unity is also important in the local church. We are to "endeavor to keep the unity of the Spirit in the bond of peace." This requires action as well as prayer. We must work to bring understanding between older and younger, traditional and modern (for example, in musical tastes), employer and employee, and between those of different ethnic backgrounds. We must work at retaining fellowship, support, and understanding between leaders in different sections of the church's life. As we work at it, we must pray. The reason for such unity is its testimony to the power of Christ among us, "that the world may believe you have sent me" (John 17:21). Similarly, the "new commandment" that we should love one another, given in John 13:34-35 is that "by this all men will know you are my disicples." So the aim of unity is not first that we may enjoy warm fellowship (even though this will be a pleasant by-product) but that the church's witness may be advanced and not blunted. The church is meant to be a non-selective collection of all sorts of people: old, young; rich, poor; healthy, sick; introvert, extrovert; single, married; intelligent, simple; fulfilled, frustrated; modern, traditional; sports-loving, book-loving; handsome, plain. Put all those together and the sparks *must* fly! If they don't fly, and if the members of such a group actually *love* one another, the only possible explanation is supernatural. It is powerful evidence of the transforming effect of belonging to Christ and being changed by his Spirit. That makes our prayer for unity more urgent, a prayer for a "seen-to-be-oneness"; that the witness of this unity may be *seen* by non-Christians, demonstrating to them the reality of Christ as living Lord among his people.

Many of us long to see the church more true to its Lord, more true to his word, more powerful in its witness, more effective in its caring, more loving in its fellowship. So let us do all *we* can as part of the church to forward these aims, but let us pray primarily for the church, locally, nationally, and internationally, that it may more and more glorify Jesus Christ, its Lord.

POSTSCRIPT

Now—over to you! This book, with all its inadequacies, is useless unless it affects the prayer-life of its readers. It has affected mine. I hope it will change yours, perhaps by a radical overhaul, or by practical action in purchasing a loose-leaf notebook and beginning a prayer diary, or by learning to "breathe" prayer, or in taking up some fresh emphasis in your praying. There is so much for us all to learn and know about the amazing privilege of praying to the God of heaven and earth, and about the effectual power of such praying, through the name of Christ and in the power of the Spirit. All prayer starts and ends with God, so:

"Rejoice in the Lord always. I will say it again: Rejoice! Do not be anxious about anything, but in everything, by prayer and petition, with thanksgiving, present your requests to God. And the peace of God, which transcends all understanding, will guard your hearts and your minds in Christ Jesus" (Phil. 4:4, 6-7; NIV).

Was this book helpful to you? Do you need insight in other areas of life? Try one or more of the following books:

The Moses Principle: Leadership and the Venture of Faith, by Michael Baughen. How God can accomplish the impossible, when we believe him. Paper. *Catalog #558-3*

Is Anyone There? (And Does It Really Matter?), by David Watson. Convincing answers for those who question the existence of God. Paper. *Catalog #395-5*

Ring of Truth: A Translator's Testimony, by J. B. Phillips. "This book ... is my testimony to the historicity and reliability of the New Testament."—J. B. Phillips. A modern classic. Paper. *Catalog #724-1*

Tell Me the Truth! by David Pawson. The truth about the essentials in the Christian world view—God, man, Christ, the Resurrectioin, the Second Coming, the Holy Spirit, sin, baptism, new life, and more. Paper. *Catalog #837-X*

So You're Single! by Margaret Clarkson. "Makes standing alone in the world a thrilling, joyful adventure."—Ann Kiemel. Paper. *Catalog #772-1*

Hereafter: What Happens After Death? by David Winter. For the bereaved and those who struggle with the fear of death. Over 100,000 in print! Paper. *Catalog #341-6*

How to Talk with God: The Dynamics of Prayer, by Stephen Winward. Chosen by Campus Life as Best Devotional Book of the Year. Over 100,000 in print! Paper. *Catalog #360-2*

How to Walk with God: Five Steps for New Christians, by David Winter. Important landmarks in the new Christian's journey. Paper. *Catalog #362-9*

How to Win the War: Strategies for Spiritual Conflict, by David Watson. How to be on the winning side in the battle with the world, the flesh, and the devil. Paper. *Catalog #308-4*

How to Listen When God Speaks: Helps for the Daily Quiet Time, by Chuck & Winnie Christensen. Whether you have five minutes or an hour to spend with God each day, this book will help you. Paper. *Catalog #355-6*

Available from your local bookstore, or
HAROLD SHAW PUBLISHERS, Box 567, Wheaton, IL 60187